# Bread Box for the Broken

*By Rebecca J. Wetzler*

PO Box 221974 Anchorage, Alaska 99522-1974
books@publicationconsultants.com—www.publicationconsultants.com

ISBN 978-1-59433-412-2

eBook ISBN Number: 978-1-59433-413-9

Copyright 2018 Rebecca J. Wetzler

Library of Congress Catalog Card Number: 2018940958

—First Edition—

Cover Image by RYC Galleries

All rights reserved, including the right of reproduction in any form, or by any mechanical or electronic means including photocopying or recording, or by any information storage or retrieval system, in whole or in part in any form, and in any case not without the written permission of the author and publisher.

Manufactured in the United States of America.

# INTRODUCTION

In John 6: 35 Jesus says "I am the bread of life. He who comes to me will never go hungry, and he who believes in me will never be thirsty." The phrase 'I am the bread of life' was a puzzling concept in Jesus' day, just as it can be for us today. To understand what the Lord is saying we must read His Word, pray for a discerning spirit, and listen as His Wisdom reveals its meaning. Scripture will make sense as the Holy Spirit opens our spiritual eyes to God's timeless Truths.

Without bread and water, we will hunger and thirst until physical starvation. To save our souls from starvation, we must have the nourishing spiritual bread and water found only in Biblical passages. As we partake of this bread, we realize our lives are full of blessings, even in our most trying circumstances. This Bread Box of Scriptures nourishes the reader's spirit through brokenness by showing trust and thanksgiving are possible despite any circumstances.

To that end, it is divided into four sections: Broken Pieces, Bread of Life, Believe in Blessings, and Bow before Him. Each section starts with the Psalms, then the scriptures are in Biblical order, i.e., Genesis, Exodus, Leviticus, etc. 'Broken Pieces' begins the prayer journey with scriptures addressing needs such as freedom from fear and perseverance through the trials. 'Bread of Life' shows God's provision and power to save. Receive encouragement from 'Believe in Blessings,' verses that tell of faith, hope and trust. Then recognize our need to 'Bow before Him' when reading about His sovereignty and giving your heart to Him in thanksgiving and obedience.

*Note: Scriptures taken from the HOLY BIBLE, NEW INTERNATIONAL VERSION (NIV) Study Bible unless otherwise annotated.*

*Copyright 1973, 1978, 1984 5th Edition International Bible Society.*

*Used by permission of Zondervan Bible Publishers (less than 1,000 verses).*

# PREFACE

This Daily Devotional *Bread Box for the Broken* was inspired more than twenty years ago by a gift from my grandmother. One Thanksgiving she gave everyone in the family a small recipe box. The words "Blessing Box" were glued to the outside lid, the verse Psalm 68:19 'Blessed be the Lord who daily loadeth us with benefits, even the Lord'(KJV) glued inside the lid. Below the scripture she stated: "WRITE DOWN YOUR BLESSINGS!" and the box contained a supply of 3 x 5 cards to do just that. Thus began the long journey of writing down 365 prayers for 365 Scriptures that have spoke to me through the years. Now complete, these scriptural prayers are intended to illustrate how Biblical truths are timeless.

The Word of God gives us strength to continue the race when we feel broken by life, and humbles us to give thanks for all the blessings along the way that often go unnoticed because of distractions. Our minds should be stayed on Him (Isaiah 26:3), for we can trust Him with our lives. As they did for me, I hope these Scripture-inspired daily prayers will bless you with hope and healing, building your confidence in His Everlasting Love for each one of us.

# Broken Pieces

# January

## 1

Dear Lord,

When reality shatters my beloved dreams, it is my own thoughts, my own agony, my own fear of the unknown that becomes my overwhelming foe. I constantly fight these negative thoughts, which tell me God will not deliver me. Hear my loud cry for deliverance I pray, and place Your shield about me. Grant me peaceful rest in body, mind and spirit so that I may lift my head, continuing my life with courage provided in Your Name.

### PSALM 3:1–6

*O Lord, how many are my foes! How many rise up against me! Many are saying of me, "God will not deliver him." But you are a shield around me, O Lord; you bestow glory on me and lift up my head. To the Lord I cry aloud, and he answers me from his holy hill. I lie down and sleep; I wake again, because the Lord sustains me. I will not fear the tens of thousands drawn up against me on every side.*

# January

# 2

### PSALM 4:1, 6–8

*Answer me when I call to you, O my righteous God. Give me relief from my distress; be merciful to me and hear my prayer ... Many are asking "who can show us any good?" Let the light of your face shine upon us, O Lord. You have filled my heart with greater joy than when their grain and new wine abound. I will lie down and sleep in peace, for you alone, O Lord, make me dwell in safety.*

Dear Lord,

As I face difficulty I pray for mercy and strength. Others will see how I withstand or how I crumble in the face of adversity—they will watch to see if good is brought into my life because I love and serve You. Grant me restful peace and resolute courage, knowing I can safely face tomorrow under Your protective wings. Let Your light shine through me, regardless of my circumstances, so that You will be glorified.

# January

# 3

## PSALM 6

Dear Lord,

How well I know these feelings! All night long I flood my bed with tears, drenching my pillow in my lonely anguish. I wonder where You are, I feel so alone. I am in agony because of my foes, whether it be other people's behavior towards me, my difficult circumstances, or the battle within for peace in my soul. My mind is full of conflicting emotions and doubt. I make mistakes; I pray for mercy that Your rebuke or discipline will not make my suffering worse, rather it will build my character and strengthen me to move past the conflicts. Please accept my prayer and lead me out of this labyrinth of despair and hopelessness.

*O Lord, do not rebuke me in your anger or discipline me in your wrath. Be merciful to me, Lord, for I am faint; O Lord heal me, for my bones are in agony. My soul is in anguish. How long, O Lord, how long? Turn, O Lord, and deliver me; save me because of your unfailing love. No one remembers you when he is dead. Who praises you from the grave? I am worn out from groaning; all night long I flood my bed with weeping and drench my couch with tears. My eyes grow weak with sorrow; they fail because of all my foes. Away from me, all you who do evil, for the Lord has heard my weeping. The Lord has heard my cry for mercy; the Lord accepts my prayer. All my enemies will be ashamed and dismayed; they will turn back in sudden disgrace.*

# January

PSALM 9:9–11

*The Lord is a refuge for the oppressed, a stronghold in times of trouble. Those who know your name will trust in you, for you, Lord, have never forsaken those who seek you. Sing praises to the Lord, enthroned in Zion; proclaim among the nations what he has done.*

Dear Lord,

There are many days I feel forsaken—I feel oppressed by the ever-present sense of deep loss, immobilized by fear of tomorrow's emptiness. I see no end in sight for the pain in my life. Help me see Your stronghold; help me seek and find refuge in Your Word, in Your Spirit, in Your Presence. I cry out to You from right where I am — bound up in my racing, suffering emotions. Lead me to that Rock that is higher than I. And as I feel You draw near, I praise and trust You with my life in these times of trouble, and of triumph.

# January

# 5

Dear Lord,

I am grieved and troubled—afflicted and oppressed by my thoughts. Victim of circumstances beyond my control, I cry out for help. Protect me from the agony caused by man and my mind. I daily commit to You the way I take; help me listen for my Father's voice that I will feel the terror no more. Give me unshakeable faith, I pray, that You will provide for my fatherless children.

## PSALM 10:14, 17–18

*But you, O God, do see trouble and grief; you consider it to take it in hand. The victim commits himself to you; you are the helper of the fatherless ... You hear, O Lord, the desire of the afflicted; you encourage them, and you listen to their cry, defending the fatherless and the oppressed, in order that man, who is of the earth, may terrify no more.*

# January

# 6

## PSALM 13

*How long O Lord? Will you forget me forever? How long will you hide your face from me? How long must I wrestle with my thoughts and every day have sorrow in my heart? How long will my enemy triumph over me? Look on me and answer, O Lord my God. Give light to my eyes, or I will sleep in death; my enemy will say, "I have overcome him," and my foes will rejoice when I fall. But I trust in your unfailing love; my heart rejoices in your salvation. I will sing to the Lord, for he has been good to me.*

Dear Lord,

"Will you forget me forever?" "How long must I wrestle with my thoughts and every day have sorrow in my heart?" These are my words Lord! How did the Psalmist know thousands of years ago I would groan these exact words from my soul? 'Wrestle with my thoughts,' that's exactly what I do. There is such a battle with an enemy within, who won't come out, rather threatens to overcome me. Yet my enemy within does not overcome—Your unfailing love sustains me through the battles. I trust in Your salvation. You have been good to me, because every day I am still standing, and you are still living in my heart, healing my sorrows.

# January

# 7

Dear Lord,

My powerful enemy, the thing too strong for me, is the battle for peace in my own soul. Days of depressive despair and unending heartache confront me, threatening to destroy me. But the Lord is my support. You reach down into my loneliness and take hold of me, assuring me You are with me in my days of disaster; and You will bring me out because You love me and I am precious in Your sight.

## PSALM 18:16–19

*He reached down from on high and took hold of me; he drew me out of deep waters. He rescued me from my powerful enemy, from my foes, who were too strong for me. They confronted me in the day of my disaster, but the Lord was my support. He brought me out into a spacious place; he rescued me because he delighted in me.*

# January

# 8

## PSALM 22:1–2, 11, 19, 24

*My God, my God, why have you forsaken me? Why are you so far from saving me, so far from the words of my groaning? O my God, I cry out by day, but you do not answer, by night, and am not silent ... Do not be far from me, for trouble is near and there is no one to help ... But you, O Lord, be not far off; O my Strength, come quickly to help me ... For he has not despised or disdained the suffering of the afflicted one; he has not hidden his face from him but has listened to his cry for help.*

Dear Lord,

There are times I feel forsaken, that You are far from saving me. I cry out, and do not hear or feel Your responding presence. There is no one else who can help me; I need You and You alone to come quickly to help me. During those times of silence I cling to the belief You are my Strength—that You know my affliction, that You are listening and will act on my behalf.

# January

## 9

### PSALM 25:15–18

*My eyes are ever on the Lord, for only he will release my feet from the snare. Turn to me and be gracious to me, for I am lonely and afflicted. The troubles of my heart have multiplied; free me from my anguish. Look upon my affliction and my distress and take away all my sins.*

Dear Lord,

What true words, the troubles of my heart have multiplied! I cannot escape the anguish of my loneliness, I cannot break free of its hold. Yes, free me from my sins—also free me from hurts not caused by my sins, rather they are just common to man. Yet they overwhelm me; in Your great mercy, free me from them all I pray.

# January

# 10

## PSALM 27:1–3

*The Lord is my light and my salvation—whom shall I fear? The Lord is the stronghold of my life—of whom shall I be afraid? When evil men advance against me to devour my flesh, when my enemies and my foes attack me, they will stumble and fall. Though an army besiege me, my heart will not fear; though war break out against me, even then will I be confident.*

Dear Lord,

Help me not to fear. You are the stronghold of my life, yet I am afraid of what some people say or do, their words shredding my confidence or my very soul. I am besieged by the loneliness and doubt of my self worth given my aloneness. I may well not let others see I am quaking in my armor, but You know. You know the battle I fight to persevere over the external and internal foes. May You be my constant light and salvation, ever present spiritual confidence.

# January

# 11

Dear Lord,

I call to You from the deep agony in my soul—forgive me of my human failings. Be merciful and guide me through to Your ways. When I feel rejected, forsaken and alone in this world, with heartache my only companion, receive me into Your presence; soothe my soul with Your peace that passes understanding. I pray You will answer me with patience, giving me once again the perseverance to continue the race known as Life.

## PSALM 27:7–10

*Hear my voice when I call, O Lord; be merciful to me and answer me. My heart says of you, "Seek his face!" Your face, Lord, I will seek. Do not hide your face from me, do not turn your servant away in anger; you have been my helper. Do not reject me or forsake me, O God my Savior. Though my father and mother forsake me, the Lord will receive me.*

# January

# 12

## PSALM 28:1, 6–7

*To you I call, O Lord my Rock; do not turn a deaf ear to me. For if you remain silent, I will be like those who have gone down to the pit ... Praise be to the Lord, for he has heard my cry for mercy. The Lord is my strength and my shield; my heart trusts in him, and I am helped. My heart leaps for joy and I will give thanks to him in song.*

Dear Lord,

I am sinking into the bottomless pit of depression; I desperately call for You Lord, I beg You do not remain silent. I know in trusting You I am helped. I worship You in song; it calms my spirit. You strengthen me for the battle, and shield my soul from succumbing to despair. I praise You for hearing my cry for You are surely the Rock on which I stand, all other ground is sinking sand.

# January

## 13

Dear Lord,

I pray for Your angels to encamp about me. I have tasted Your goodness, and seek refuge in You. Help me feel that protection, and understand I lack no good thing, even though it may seem my world is collapsing about me. For ultimately, by faith, I am delivered from eternal death to everlasting life. Your Salvation is the most important good thing of all. I seek to follow Your goodness, keeping evil out of my life, speaking truth to others so they may know You through my words and actions. I seek Your peace that it will be manifest within me.

### PSALM 34:7–14

*The angel of the Lord encamps around those who fear him, and he delivers them. Taste and see that the Lord is good; blessed is the man who takes refuge in him. Fear the Lord, you his saints, for those who fear him lack nothing. The lions may grow weak and hungry, but those who seek the Lord lack no good thing. Come, my children, listen to me; I will teach you the fear of the Lord. Whoever of you loves life and desires to see many good days, keep your tongue from evil and your lips from speaking lies. Turn from evil and do good; seek peace and pursue it.*

# January

# 14

PSALM 34:19–22

*A righteous man may have many troubles, but the Lord delivers him from them all; he protects all his bones, not one of them will be broken. Evil will slay the wicked; the foes of the righteous will be condemned. The Lord redeems his servants; no one will be condemned who takes refuge in him.*

Dear Lord,

I do not feel righteous, I do not feel good enough to ask for Your deliverance, but I have many troubles. Then Your Holy Spirit reminds me that You are my righteousness, you have washed my soul with the precious blood of Jesus Christ. You have redeemed me through His resurrection, and You see I sincerely seek to be Your servant through faith in Your Word. Thank you for giving me refuge rather than condemnation. I praise You for the deliverance that comes from You and You alone.

# January

# 15

Dear Lord,

You know the longings of my heart; You know how it hurts, how my spirit sighs in unbearable pain as my longings go unfulfilled year after year. My strength to persevere fails me, and without the light of your hope, I may fall into sin or worse … I pray for your merciful forgiveness—please do not forsake me in my time of unrelenting heartbreak, weakened to the point of searching for fulfillment where there is none. Come quickly, for just as the psalmist, I feel my heart pound, the light going from my eyes, my very breath is weak. But praise God, I know You are my help and my portion from beginning to end.

PSALM 38:9–10, 17–18, 21–22

*All my longings lie open before you, O Lord; my sighing is not hidden from you. My heart pounds, my strength fails me; even the light has gone from my eyes … For I am about to fall, and my pain is ever with me. I confess my iniquity; I am troubled by my sin … O Lord, do not forsake me; be not far from me, O my God. Come quickly to help me, O Lord my Savior.*

# January

# 16

## PSALM 40:1–3

*I waited patiently for the Lord; he turned to me and heard my cry. He lifted me out of the slimy pit, out of the mud and mire; he set my feet on a rock and gave me a firm place to stand. He put a new song in my mouth, a hymn of praise to our God. Many will see and fear and put their trust in the Lord.*

Dear Lord,

My fears, failures, frustrations are like miry clay, sucking me down into the depths of the cares of this life. You hear my cry for deliverance, You give me confidence I will overcome through You. Because of my faith in Your goodness and mercy You lift me to solid ground. When I am bowed down under the weight of the world, You gently take it from me so I may stand in praise of Your Holy Name. I put my trust in You to calm my fears; teach me from my failures, encourage me through my frustrations, and forever hold my soul safely in Your loving hands.

# January

# 17

## PSALM 40:11–13

*Do not withhold your mercy from me, O Lord; may your love and your truth always protect me. For troubles without number surround me; my sins have overtaken me, and I cannot see. They are more than the hairs of my head, and my heart fails within me. Be pleased, O Lord, to save me; O Lord, come quickly to help me.*

Dear Lord,

When I feel overwhelmed by failure and/or seemingly insurmountable obstacles, whether they be a result of my own foolish folly or just because the world can be a cruel place, I need Your mercy and love. Despite the innumerable troubles I seem to face, I pray Your Truth, eternal peace through my Savior Jesus Christ, will protect me from doubts and discouragements. But when I am overcome by them, I pray Your Word will quickly speak the Truth to my spirit to save me. Then the sin or sorrow which has overtaken me will fade in light of Your great mercy.

# January

# 18

## PSALM 43:2–5

*You are God my stronghold. Why have you rejected me? Why must I go about mourning, oppressed by the enemy? Send forth your light and your truth, let them guide me; let them bring me to your holy mountain, to the place where you dwell. Then will I go to the altar of God, to God, my joy and my delight. I will praise you with the harp, O God, my God. Why are you downcast, O my soul? Why so disturbed within me? Put your hope in God, for I will yet praise him, my Savior and my God.*

Dear Lord,

You are my stronghold. So why does it sometimes feel like you have rejected me? That you allow me to continually be oppressed by my enemies: worries of my mind, hurts in my heart, and the accompanying manifestation of physical pain? Give me hope and wisdom from Your Word, my Light in this darkness. Guide me to where once again Your peace and presence dwell within my heart and soul so I am no longer downcast and disturbed. Help me lay these burdens on Your altar, trusting You will deliver me as I praise You.

# January

# 19

Dear Lord,

I have storms in my life that make me feel like the world is disintegrating about me; similar to the roar of a strong mountain tumbling into the foaming, devouring sea. Help me not to fear, despite the overwhelming intensity of a storm. Rather remind me You are ever-present in my life, a constant source of solid strength, a safe haven where I may ride out any storm in the safety and comfort of the Everlasting Arms. Within each storm, I pray for a river of mercy to flow into my heart, renewing me daily with the love of God.

## PSALM 46:1–5

*God is our refuge and strength, an ever-present help in trouble. Therefore we will not fear, though the earth give way and the mountains fall into the heart of the sea, though its waters roar and foam and the mountains quake with their surging. There is a river whose streams make glad the city of God, the holy place where the Most High dwells. God is within her, she will not fall; God will help her at break of day.*

# January

# 20

## PSALM 55:16–19, 22

*But I call to God, and the Lord saves me. Evening, morning and noon I cry out in distress, and he hears my voice. He ransoms me unharmed from the battle waged against me, even though many oppose me. God, who is enthroned forever, will hear them and afflict them—men who never change their ways and have no fear of God ... Cast your cares on the Lord and he will sustain you; he will never let the righteous fall.*

Dear Lord,

Many things oppose me, seen and unseen. From early to late I silently cry out my distress to You; yet I still need to function efficiently in my daily life. I cast my cares upon You, and You always hear my voice. You carry me through uncertain days. You will sustain me through the struggle or ransom me from the difficulty. In either case You never fail me, You are my Lord who saves me and blesses me in all things.

# January

# 21

Dear Lord,

You know every tear I shed, You have record of every reason why they fall. When mortal man hurts me to the core, You know and are near in my brokenness. When I am afraid the hurt will never heal, I trust in You to see me through, hoping someday for full deliverance. In the meantime, I praise You that although loneliness attempts to consume me, You are ever with me in this solitude; Your Holy Spirit dispels the closing darkness and Your constant Presence gives me hope in yesterday, today and tomorrow.

### PSALM 56:3–4,8–11

*When I am afraid, I will trust in you. In God, whose word I praise, in God I trust; I will not be afraid. What can mortal man do to me? … Record my lament; list my tears on your scroll—are they not in your record? Then my enemies will turn back when I call for help. By this I will know that God is for me. In God, whose word I praise, in the Lord, whose word I praise—in God I trust; I will not be afraid. What can man do to me?*

# January

# 22

## PSALM 57:1–3

*Have mercy on me, O God, have mercy on me, for in you my soul takes refuge. I will take refuge in the shadow of your wings until the disaster has passed. I cry out to God Most High, to God who fulfills his purpose for me. He sends from heaven and saves me, rebuking those who hotly pursue me; God sends his love and his faithfulness.*

Dear Lord,

When trials and tribulations hotly pursue me, remind me Your love and faithfulness do not fail me. Hide my soul safely in the shadow of Your wings until the disaster passes—do not let my human despair lose touch with Your merciful presence. Help me still fulfill Your purpose for my life, no matter how great the disappointments or obstacles I face; remind me when I am losing hope, that You are my ever present refuge within. I am confident Your mercy covers my life and Your Spirit leads me forward in victory and peace.

# January

# 23

## PSALM 61:1–5

Dear Lord,

I grow weary fighting the unseen foes that assail my heart and mind. I feel abandoned, alone and defenseless. Please hear my cry for help—I feel like I am at the end, praying desperately for refuge from the battle. You are my Rock above the waves of war threatening to overcome my faint heart; I pray You bring me into the safe haven of Your towering strength. You have heard my vows to serve and follow You all the days of my life; You have given me a heritage as Your child, one of mercy and hope, eternal protection for my soul and the compassionate grace of Your Spirit living in me. I know You hear my prayers and You have delivered me.

*Hear my cry, O God; listen to my prayer. From the ends of the earth I call to you, I call as my heart grows faint; lead me to the rock that is higher than I. For you have been my refuge, a strong tower against the foe. I long to dwell in your tent forever and take refuge in the shelter of your wings. For you have heard my vows, O God; you have given me the heritage of those who fear your name.*

# January

# 24

PSALM 66:16–20

*Come and listen, all you who fear God; let me tell you what he has done for me. I cried out to him with my mouth; his praise was on my tongue. If I had cherished sin in my heart, the Lord would not have listened; but God has surely listened and heard my voice in prayer. Praise be to God, who has not rejected my prayer or withheld his love from me!*

Dear Lord,

I cry out to You from my heart, and praise You for Your constant presence within my soul. Though I may stumble through sin along my way, as I pray humbly for forgiveness, I believe You know I truly cherish Your Way. Because I have the indwelling of the Holy Spirit through Christ, I know You love me and are faithful to forgive. I praise You for always listening to my sincere prayers, and tirelessly leading me as I seek to follow Your Will for my life. Let me tell others what You have done for me: You are my Comforter, my Provider, my Healer, my ever-present Help. You are the Alpha and Omega. Most important of all, You are my Everlasting Savior.

# January

# 25

## PSALM 69:1–3

*Save me, O God, for the waters have come up to my neck. I sink in the miry depths, where there is no foothold. I have come into the deep waters; the floods engulf me. I am worn out calling for help; my throat is parched. My eyes fail, looking for my God.*

Dear Lord,

I am sinking deep into the miry depths of depression—I cannot get a foothold to stop my descent. I am worn out calling for help—desperately looking about me for You to appear. Rescue me I pray, before I am engulfed completely by failure, by sorrow, by isolation. Pull me into Your protective, peaceful presence so I may rest amidst these storms that assail my soul. Restore me so I know my confidence is in You and not what goes on about me, nor my ability to deal with it. You are my strength, You are my portion; You feed and water my soul with Your Word, empowering me to follow the footholds of faith, until I am once again standing on solid ground with my Lord and Savior.

# January

# 26

PSALM 69:5–6, 13–14

*You know my folly, O God; my guilt is not hidden from you. May those who hope in you not be disgraced because of me, O Lord, the Lord Almighty; may those who seek you not be put to shame because of me, O God of Israel ... But I pray to you, O Lord, in the time of your favor; in your great love, O God, answer me with your sure salvation. Rescue me from the mire, do not let me sink; deliver me from those who hate me, from the deep waters.*

Dear Lord,

Please keep others from being discouraged or disillusioned with You because of my folly, my guilt of sinful behavior. All have sinned and come short of the glory of God, believers and non-believers both. You know I humbly pray for forgiveness, You rescue me from sinking further in the miry clay of sin, though the battle may be long. At the times I stumble, help others to look towards You, not me. Always may they look beyond this human frailty; instead may they see Your image steadily shining through brighter and brighter the longer I walk with You.

# January

# 27

## PSALM 69:16–20

Dear Lord,

I pray for Your great mercy to rescue me from my troubles. Some are circumstances, other are consequences; some are out of my control, others I fail to control. I pray You do not hide Your face from me in the turmoil. I scorn myself when I am not the woman of God You have called me to be, when I have not shown others what Jesus would do. Instead I shame Your Holy Name by poor reactions or inactions. Be near me and show me Your Way, quickly, so my brokenness may find peace, safety, and healing in You. Remind me again to handle life prayerfully. In You alone I find sympathy and help for all my struggles, self-inflicted or when caught in crossfire, and I praise Your goodness to me.

*Answer me, O Lord, out of the goodness of your love; in your great mercy turn to me. Do not hide your face from your servant; answer me quickly, for I am in trouble. Come near and rescue me; redeem me because of my foes. You know how I am scorned, disgraced and shamed; all my enemies are before you. Scorn has broken my heart and has left me helpless; I looked for sympathy, but there was none, for comforters, but I found none.*

# January

# 28

### PSALM 71;17–21

*Since my youth, O God, you have taught me, and to this day I declare your marvelous deeds. Even when I am old and gray, do not forsake me, O God, till I declare your power to the next generation, your might to all who are to come. Your righteousness reaches to the skies, O God, you who have done great things. Who, O God, is like you? Though you have made me see troubles, many and bitter, you will restore my life again; from the depths of the earth you will again bring me up. You will increase my honor and comfort me once again.*

Dear Lord,

I have seen troubles, many and bitter; in spite of them I have loved You from my youth. I have come through all of them knowing You are teaching me invaluable lessons and You repeatedly restore my faith and strengthen my resolve to continue the race. Your priceless Wisdom is worth the depths of despair, as they ultimately must give way to the marvelous works you are doing in my life. I pray, as I grow to be old and gray, those who know me will continually see Your unmistakable imprint throughout my life, bringing knowledge to their hearts there is none like You.

# January

## 29

### PSALM 73:3–5, 11–17

*For I envied the arrogant when I saw the prosperity of the wicked. They have no struggles; their bodies are healthy and strong. They are free from burdens common to man; they are not plagued by human ills ... They say, "How can God know? Does the Most High have knowledge?" This is what the wicked are like — always carefree, they increase in wealth. Surely in vain have I kept my heart pure; in vain have I washed my hands in innocence. All day long I have been plagued; I have been punished every morning. If I had said, "I will speak thus," I would have betrayed your children. When I tried to understand all this, it was oppressive to me till I entered the sanctuary of God; then I understood their final destiny.*

Dear Lord,

Forgive me, but I find myself envious of those who appear to ignore Your Sovereignty, Your very existence, yet they still prosper while I struggle emotionally, physically and financially. And all the while I do my best to follow the Savior of my soul who has promised an eternity in heaven with Him. The others, however, follow worldly things and prosper, even mock You. But are they really prospering? Your Spirit reminds me they are bound for an eternity without You. It is then I understand; while without the storms of life may rage, I am safe within Your sanctuary. They are being deceived by carefree living, without knowledge of the coming spiritual storm where they will be lost without Your sanctuary.

# January

# 30

### PSALM 86:1–4

*Hear, O Lord, and answer me, for I am poor and needy. Guard my life, for I am devoted to you. You are my God; save your servant who trusts in you. Have mercy on me, O Lord, for I call to you all day long. Bring joy to your servant, for to you, O Lord, I lift up my soul.*

Dear Lord,

I am devoted to You; my thoughts continually return to You throughout the day. Thankful thoughts for the daily blessings, anxious thoughts as I call on Your mercy moment by moment. I need Your strength to overcome my many fears, both real and imagined. I pray You guard my soul against overwhelming anxiety, depression, loneliness; the fears that crush my spirit as I struggle through this world alone. Yet I am not alone, for You are with me; my Provider when I am poor, my Comforter when I am needy, my Healer when I am sick or in pain. I am eternally grateful You carry me through it all every time I call to You. Because of Your mercy, I can trust You in all things. I give my life as a thank offering, praying for You to mold me into Your will that I may serve Your purposes.

# January

# 31

## PSALM 91:1–6,14–15

*He who dwells in the shelter of the Most High will rest in the shadow of the Almighty. I will say of the Lord, "He is my refuge and my fortress, my God, in whom I trust." Surely he will save you from the fowler's snare and from the deadly pestilence. He will cover you with his feathers, and under his wings you will find refuge; his faithfulness will be your shield and rampart. You will not fear the terror of night, nor the arrow that flies by day, nor the pestilence that stalks in the darkness, nor the plague that destroys at midday … ."Because he loves me," says the Lord, "I will rescue him; I will protect him, for he acknowledges my name. He will call upon me, and I will answer him; I will be with him in trouble, I will deliver him and honor him."*

Dear Lord,

You know I love You. You know I acknowledge and gratefully accept You as the All-Mighty God, Christ my Savior, and the indwelling of the Holy Spirit. Rescue me from the overwhelming pain in my heart and soul. Be my refuge, my fortress in this turbulent time. Hide me under Your protective wing, safe from the attacks of sorrow encircling me throughout the day, and the threatening terror of another fearful night alone and unloved. Thank You for Your Word that says because I love You, You will rescue and protect me; that when I call upon You, You are ever near. Your Presence shields me from the enemy's cycle of pain and it pierces the lonely darkness with Your glorious light of love.

# February

## 1

### PSALM 107:28–31

*Then they cried out to the Lord in their trouble, and he brought them out of their distress. He stilled the storm to a whisper; the waves of the sea were hushed. They were glad when it grew calm, and he guided them to their desired haven. Let them give thanks to the Lord for his unfailing love and his wonderful deeds for men.*

Dear Lord,

I cry out in my trouble—I scream and plead and beg You to end the hysteria rising within my spirit, threatening to swallow me in its dark madness. I cling to Your Word that You bring the storm to a whisper, and guide me to my desired haven—Your peaceful presence. I am so grateful for that calm only You can give. Your Spirit reminds me of all the wonderful deeds You have done in my life, then my spirit is hushed, returning to the comfort of trusting You with my circumstances. I am humbled by Your patience with me in my struggle with dark feelings and fears. Thank you from the deepest part of my soul for Your unfailing love.

# February

## 2

Dear Lord,

Like the psalmist, I am overcome by trouble and sorrow. I become so entangled in my emotions, it's like a fate worse than death. Help me know You hear my cry for mercy; help me feel You calm my spirit; help me rest in the peace of Your salvation. Because of Your great compassion, let Your love reign in my heart where anguish has held me captive. May I live no longer as a captive, rather enable me to honor You with a simple life, well-lived for You, my Savior.

### PSALM 116:1–6

*I love the Lord, for he heard my voice; he heard my cry for mercy. Because he turned his ear to me, I will call on him as long as I live. The cords of death entangled me, the anguish of the grave came upon me; I was overcome by trouble and sorrow. Then I called on the name of the Lord, "O Lord, save me!" The Lord is gracious and righteous; our God is full of compassion. The Lord protects the simple-hearted; when I was in great need, he saved me.*

# February

## 3

### PSALM 118:1, 5–12

*Give thanks to the Lord, for he is good; his love endures forever … . In my anguish I cried to the Lord, and he answered by setting me free. The Lord is with me; I will not be afraid. What can man do to me? The Lord is with me; he is my helper. I will look in triumph on my enemies. It is better to take refuge in the Lord than to trust in man. It is better to take refuge in the Lord than to trust in princes. All the nations surrounded me, but in the name of the Lord I cut them off. They surrounded me on every side, but in the name of the Lord I cut them off. They swarmed around me like bees, but they died out as quickly as burning thorns; in the name of the Lord I cut them off.*

Dear Lord,

I have been deeply hurt by others, my anguish too deep to share with anyone but You. Only You can set me free to live again, to reach within where Your Spirit dwells to risk yet another injury. Help me not be afraid, even when I am exposed to painful situations where others can discourage or harm my spirit with unknowing or thoughtless words and actions. I must trust in You rather than anyone around me to give me my worth. I will look to You, my Savior and Help in time of trouble. When painful thoughts and feelings swarm me like bees, heal their stings quickly so I am not cut off from life, rather I am alive under the protection of Your Name. You are always with me—I trust in Your enduring love to give me the victory.

# February

Dear Lord,

Thank you for convicting me of my sin; I stray in the wrong direction more times than I ever thought I would. Though I may face difficult consequences for breaking my covenant with You, You are forever my salvation and righteousness. Chastened and contrite for failing You yet again, You accept my sincere plea and forgive me, yet again. Your sacrifice on the cross provides all sinners the cleansing blood to wash away the world's filth, and instead covers us with Your righteousness. No words adequately express my thankfulness that You are the Answer for all of life's questions, though I may not learn of it until I humbly bow at Your feet. I will bow in eternal gratitude that You have allowed me to enter into Your Holy Gates, and I will sing Your praises forever.

## PSALM 118:17–21

*I will not die but live, and will proclaim what the Lord has done. The Lord has chastened me severely, but he has not given me over to death. Open for me the gates of righteousness; I will enter and give thanks to the Lord. This is the gate of the Lord through which the righteous may enter. I will give you thanks, for you answered me; you have become my salvation.*

# February

# 5

## PSALM 119:145–149

*I call with all my heart; answer me, O Lord, and I will obey your decrees. I call out to you; save me and I will keep your statutes. I rise before dawn and cry for help; I have put my hope in your word. My eyes stay open through the watches of the night, that I may meditate on your promises. Hear my voice in accordance with your love; preserve my life, O Lord, according to your laws. Those who devise wicked schemes are near, but they are far from your law. Yet you are near, O Lord, and all your commands are true. Long ago I learned from your statutes that you established them to last forever.*

Dear Lord,

You know the countless nights I lay awake in bed, crying out to You my fears, my worries, my needs, my broken dreams, desperately needing Your help. Through Your Spirit, I pray no sin rule over me nor any anxiety separate me from feeling Your presence; I know only You can direct my steps in the way that preserves my life. Therefore I will ever meditate on Your promises of deliverance and peace as I sincerely serve You. Long ago in my childhood You revealed Yourself to me as my Savior, and I know You are near me as I walk through this life.

# February

# 6

Dear Lord,

The night can be such a lonely time; darkness only intensifies the feelings of loneliness. Help me know I am not alone. I need to lift up my eyes, past the hills of my problems to Your heavenly sanctuary, and then I know Your Spirit is with me. Help me know You are constantly watching over me, and I may slumber peacefully in the darkness, knowing You remain wide awake.

## PSALM 121:1–4

*I lift up my eyes to the hills—where does my help come from? My help comes from the Lord, the Maker of heaven and earth. He will not let your foot slip—he who watches over you will not slumber; indeed, he who watches over Israel will neither slumber nor sleep.*

# February

# 7

## PSALM 121:5–8

*The Lord watches over you—the Lord is your shade at your right hand; the sun will not harm you by day, nor the moon by night. The Lord will keep you from all harm—he will watch over your life; the Lord will watch over your coming and going both now and forevermore.*

Dear Lord,

Sometimes it is hard believe you are always watching over me, keeping me from harm. Because I do come into harm's way, despite my efforts to stay in the shade of Your Spirit. I get bruised and broken, becoming weak and descending into despair. Why, why do I suffer if you are watching over me? Then You help me understand Yours is the everlasting watch—no matter the harms that may come my way here on earth, my soul is eternally watched and kept safe by Your grace and power as I keep my faith and trust in You.

# February

# 8

Dear Lord,

My grief is too deep to express. My house and home are destroyed, for not all the builders looked to You for the spiritual materials required. I watched in vain, unable to guard that which had been entrusted to me, forgive my failure I pray. I look at my small children and weep uncontrollably, how will I provide for them now? I am weary to the bone, but my mind and my emotions won't let me be; they torment me from early morning to the late watches of the night. Yet I know You are with me, holding me up or surely I will perish. Please grant me sleep so I may have strength of mind, body and soul for the difficult days ahead; I know my salvation from all things lies in You alone.

## PSALM 127:1–2

*Unless the Lord builds the house, its builders labor in vain. Unless the Lord watches over the city, the watchmen stand guard in vain. In vain you rise early and stay up late, toiling for food to eat—for he grants sleep to those he loves.*

# February

## 9

### PSALM 139:7–12

*Where can I go from your Spirit? Where can I flee from your presence? If I go up to the heavens, you are there; if I make my bed in the depths, you are there. If I rise on the wings of the dawn, if I settle on the far side of the sea, even there your hand will guide me, your right hand will hold me fast. If I say, "Surely the darkness will hide me and the light become night around me," even the darkness will not be dark to you; the night will shine like the day, for darkness is as light to you.*

Dear Lord,

Sometimes I am so discouraged and disappointed that I just want to hide from You. I cannot measure up, this life is too hard, I keep failing. But then Your Word reminds me there is no where You are not. When I am in the deepest depression, You are in the depths to bring me back out; when I feel far removed, invisible to those around me, You guide me through the loneliness with the comfort of Your everlasting presence. When I cannot see worth in myself, You remind me long ago You laid Your hand upon my life because You have a special purpose just for me. You shine hope into my soul that You are not done with me, and the darkness retreats from Your Holy Light.

# February

# 10

**PSALM 139:15–16**

*My frame was not hidden from you when I was made in the secret place. When I was woven together in the depths of the earth, your eyes saw my unformed body. All the days ordained for me were written in your book before one of them came to be.*

Dear Lord,

I do not know what the future holds. There are days I look forward to tomorrow, days I dread what I know I must go through, and days I fear I cannot face the unknown one more time. You saw me before I was even formed; You wove my being together—my physical body, my personality, my spirit and planted my soul. So my fears are not hidden from You when they lurk in the deepest places of my heart. When I call upon You, You are already there within my spirit to calm its trembling. You remind me You know all my yesterdays, where I am today, and where I will go tomorrow—You have written my life's path for Your glory, and it is for me to follow You faithfully into eternity.

# February

# 11

## PSALM 142:1–7

*I cry aloud to the Lord; I lift up my voice to the Lord of mercy. I pour out my complaint before him; before him I tell my trouble. When my spirit grows faint within me, it is you who know my way. In the path where I walk men have hidden a snare for me. Look to my right and see; no one is concerned for me. I have no refuge; no one cares for my life. I cry to you, O Lord; I say, "You are my refuge, my portion in the land of the living." Listen to my cry, for I am in desperate need; rescue me from those who pursue me, for they are too strong for me. Set me free from my prison, that I may praise your name. Then the righteous will gather about me because of your goodness to me.*

Dear Lord,

Many a night I lift my voice to You in desperate prayer, crying out my complaints, my sorrows, my grief for lost dreams. My spirit is faint within me, and I do not know how I can continue living with my pain, not knowing the hidden snares ahead that will further destroy me. I often feel invisible, no one concerned about the burdens I carry alone. I beg of You to free me from my prison of loneliness, depression, grief, helplessness, uselessness. You know my way out; You know there is a purpose for these difficulties. I need Your help to bear them in a more effective way, the way that honors You. I praise Your name for who You are, regardless of life's challenges, for with You I am forever free.

# February

## 12

Dear Lord,

My humble plea for mercy is continuous, never ending. I am eternally grateful that You always hear my prayer, always cover me with Your righteousness, always exemplify the faithfulness that the created should have for the Creator. Through each of life's lessons You walk with me. Through grace You deliver Your servant from judgment and my transgressions are forgiven; by Your Spirit I go forward stronger than before, once again delivered from my internal enemies by my Lord and Savior.

### PSALM 143:1–2

*O Lord, hear my prayer, listen to my cry for mercy; in your faithfulness and righteousness come to my relief. Do not bring your servant into judgment, for no one living is righteous before you.*

# February

# 13

## PSALM 143:3–6

*The enemy pursues me, he crushes me to the ground; he makes me dwell in darkness like those long dead. So my spirit grows faint within me; my heart within me is dismayed. I remember the days of long ago; I meditate on all your works and consider what your hands have done. I spread out my hands to you; my soul thirsts for you like a parched land.*

Dear Lord,

My spirit grows faint within me, dismayed and worn down by the enemies of my mind, heart and soul. Stress pursues me, pain crushes my resilience, depression looms before me ready to swallow me into its darkness. But then, I remember the past battles won; each and every one were overcome by faith in Your goodness. I will meditate on Your Word and on what you have done for me in the past, see what you are doing today, and believe in what you will do in the future. I spread my life before You, resolved to follow You through to more victories over darkness. Only fellowship with You will quench my thirst for peace in my heart, soul and mind.

# February

# 14

Dear Lord,

I need to feel Your presence now, every day, every minute, every second. My spirit fails within me, my soul despairs in darkness as I lift it to You for healing. Renew my soul I pray, just like a glorious morning dawns after a torturous storm has raged through the night. I fear my troubled soul can endure no more; but I trust in Your unfailing love to show me the way through the blackness to Your glorious light. No longer will the darkness keep me hidden from Your sight; rather I hide myself in You. You place me on level ground, giving me respite from the trials of life. It is my heart's desire to be Your humble servant, continually learning and following in Your way.

## PSALM 143:7–12

*Answer me quickly O Lord; my spirit fails. Do not hide your face from me or I will be like those who go down to the pit. Let the morning bring me word of your unfailing love, for I have put my trust in you. Show me the way I should go, for to you I lift up my soul. Rescue me from my enemies, O Lord, for I hide myself in you. Teach me to do your will, for you are my God; may your good Spirit lead me on level ground. For your name's sake, O Lord, preserve my life; in your righteousness, bring me out of trouble. In your unfailing love, silence my enemies; destroy all my foes, for I am your servant.*

# February

# 15

## NUMBERS 23:19–21

*God is not a man, that he should lie, nor a son of man, that he should change his mind. Does he speak and then not act? Does he promise and not fulfill? I have received a command to bless; he has blessed, and I cannot change it. No misfortune is seen in Jacob, no misery observed in Israel. The Lord their God is with them: the shout of the King is among them.*

Dear Lord,

Thank you that You are not like us. We change our minds with the direction of the wind when what we need is to stay the course ahead; we speak lofty talk, yet little action; we may be full of promises in time of crises yet leave them forgotten and unfulfilled once immediate deliverance has come; we may lie when we think the ends justifies the means. No; You Lord, are unchanged age to age, ever faithful. You speak it, and it is so. Your commands are carried out in Your time. Today and every day I set my mind towards You. I pray my faith in You does not change in the battle, rather it be strengthened by every misfortune and misery You bring me through.

# February

# 16

## DEUTERONOMY
### 30:19–20B, 31:6

Dear Lord,

Life terrifies me at times. I do not know how to go on with the fear of tomorrow because I can hardly make it through today. Thank you for Your Word that tells me You are my life, my reason for living. You have gone before me into tomorrow so I can be strong today. I can face life with courage, knowing You will never forsake me and my children. And when it is all over, heaven waits where forevermore there is no more fear, no more pain, and no more tears.

*[Moses said] "This day I call the heavens and the earth as witnesses against you that I have set before you life and death, blessings and curses. Now choose life; so that you and your children may live and that you may love the Lord your God, listen to his voice, and hold fast to him. For the Lord is your life, ... Be strong and courageous. Do not be afraid or terrified because of them, for the Lord your God goes with you; he will never leave you nor forsake you."*

# February

# 17

## DEUTERONOMY
## 33:26–27

*There is no one like the God of Jeshurun, who rides on the heavens to help you and on the clouds in his majesty. The eternal God is your refuge, and underneath are the everlasting arms. He will drive out your enemy before you, saying, "Destroy him!"*

Dear Lord,

How I need to feel Your Everlasting Arms comforting me! How I need to reach the refuge of Your presence! My enemy is intangible; it attacks my mind, my heart, my spirit. I have asked You to "Destroy him," yet the attacks continue. I pray You continue driving out the enemy no matter how many times it returns. Help me know we will prevail together.

# February

# 18

## JOSHUA 1:7–9

Dear Lord,

I get discouraged, and once in a while, down-right petrified of life's circumstances. Thank you the Bible tells of historical believers who experienced the same. Just like them, may I draw on Your strength for the courage to go forth into the unknown. For though it is unknown to me, it is not unknown to You. As I meditate on Your Word, You speak peace to my spirit. Though I may not be prosperous by the world's definition, I am prosperous in the things of God when I listen to Your commands. Your commands are not burdensome; they are my way to successfully navigate this chaotic world with You by my side everywhere I go.

*"Be strong and very courageous. Be careful to obey all the law my servant Moses gave you; do not turn from it to the right or to the left, that you may be successful wherever you go. Do not let this Book of the Law depart from your mouth; meditate on it day and night, so that you may be careful to do everything written in it. Then you will be prosperous and successful. Have I not commanded you? Be strong and courageous. Do not be terrified; do not be discouraged, for the Lord your God will be with you wherever you go."*

# February

# 19

## II SAMUEL 22:17–23

*He reached down from on high and took hold of me; he drew me out of deep waters. He rescued me from my powerful enemy, from my foes, who were too strong for me. They confronted me in the day of my disaster, but the Lord was my support. He brought me out into a spacious place; he rescued me because he delighted in me. The Lord has dealt with me according to my righteousness; according to the cleanness of my hands he has rewarded me. For I have kept the ways of the Lord; I have not done evil by turning from my God. All his laws are before me; I have not turned away from his decrees.*

Dear Lord,

I so desperately need You to rescue me from my powerful enemy. The battle for my mind wages endlessly, and I fear my unseen foe is too strong for me. It confronts me day and night; renew my hope in Your deliverance. Please be my support, bring me out of this dungeon of depression into Your spacious light of peace. I keep to Your way; when I sin against Your Word, I humbly and sincerely ask for forgiveness. Reach down from Your throne on High, pull me safely out of my real and imagined disasters so I may be Your effective servant.

# February

# 20

Dear Lord,

It is so true only You know the hearts of men. It is only to You that I may plead for deliverance from my deepest fears and my most aching unfulfilled longings. My spirit stretches out towards You again and again, needing that calming touch only You can give. I need to hear from You. Then I know You are aware of my afflictions and pains, and You will carry me through all of them as I walk in Your ways.

## II CHRONICLES 6:29–31

*... and when a prayer or plea is made by any of your people Israel—each one aware of his afflictions and pains, and spreading out his hands toward this temple—then [you] hear from heaven, your dwelling place. Forgive, and deal with each man according to all he does, since you know his heart (for you alone know the hearts of men), so that they will fear you and walk in your ways all the time they live in the land you gave our fathers.*

# February

# 21

## II CHRONICLES 6:36–39

*When they sin against you—for there is no one who does not sin—and you become angry with them and give them over to the enemy, who takes them captive to a land far away or near; and if they have a change of heart in the land where they are held captive, and repent and plead with you in the land of their captivity and say, "We have sinned, we have done wrong and acted wickedly;" and if they turn back to you with all their heart and soul in the land of their captivity where they were taken, and pray toward the land you gave their fathers, toward the city you have chosen and toward the temple I have built in your Name; then from heaven, your dwelling place, hear their prayer and their pleas, and uphold their cause. And forgive your people, who have sinned against you.*

Dear Lord,

To err is human; it is not 'if' I sin it is 'when' will I sin again. When I am taken over by the deceit of the enemy, You may well be angry with my behavior—and allow me to be captive to the error of my ways. Yet when I turn back to You, humbly asking for forgiveness, You will faithfully uphold Your promise to forgive, never for a moment having stopped loving me. I may still have consequences to deal with, however I am free from the sin that binds. I do not have to go to a temple to meet with You, for I have built a temple in my heart for You to dwell.

# February

# 22

## II CHRONICLES
20:3,12,15

Dear Lord,

How many times, just like Jehoshaphat, I am alarmed by too vast an enemy! I do not know how to turn aside the battle for my heart and mind. Broken dreams, depression, fears, emotional and physical pain attack me daily. Help me resolve to reach out to You in quiet prayer so You may calm my spirit, and remind me the battle is Yours. I need only entrust victory to You, following Your lead as I pass through the valley.

*Alarmed, Jehoshaphat resolved to inquire of the Lord, and he proclaimed a fast for all Judah … "O our God, will you not judge them? For we have no power to face this vast army that is attacking us. We do not know what to do, but our eyes are upon you" … He [Jahaziel, son of Zechariah] said: "Listen, King Jehoshaphat and all who live in Judah and Jerusalem! This is what the Lord says to you: 'Do not be afraid or discouraged because of this vast army. For the battle is not yours, but God's.'"*

# February

# 23

## II CHRONICLES
32:7–8

*"Be strong and courageous. Do not be afraid or discouraged because of the king of Assyria and the vast army with him, for there is a greater power with us than with him. With him is only the arm of flesh, but with us is the Lord our God to help us and to fight our battles." And the people gained confidence from what Hezekiah the king of Judah said.*

Dear Lord,

It is very hard to be strong and courageous when the enemy is vast; when overwhelming troubles come from without; when the emotional pain within affects my ability to breathe. Thank you for the reminder that You fight my battles for me. Quiet my fears, I pray; distill my discouragement with the knowledge that You are the Greatest Power.

# February

# 24

Dear Lord,

How well I understand the statement 'man is born to trouble.' Likewise, how well I understand that when I appeal to You, You perform wonders that cannot be fathomed. Daily I lay my cause before You, desperate for You to water my soul with peace. As I spend time with You in my thoughts, thank you You set my lowly feelings back to emotional and spiritual safety.

## JOB 5:7–11

*Yet man is born to trouble as surely as sparks fly upward. But if it were I, I would appeal to God; I would lay my cause before him. He performs wonders that cannot be fathomed, miracles that cannot be counted. He bestows rain on the earth; he sends water upon the countryside. The lowly he sets on high, and those who mourn are lifted to safety.*

# February

# 25

### JOB 23:10–12

*But he knows the way I take; when he has tested me, I will come forth as gold. My feet have closely followed his steps; I have kept to his way without turning aside. I have not departed from the commands of his lips; I have treasured the words of his mouth more than my daily bread.*

Dear Lord,

At times I am so fearful of what lay ahead of me—I find so much comfort knowing You know the way I take. Though I stumble and even fall, I do not turn aside from the goal of following my Lord Jesus Christ. I treasure Your Word, for though it was written centuries before I was born, it speaks hope to me personally every day.

# February

# 26

## JOB 26:1–3, 14

*Then Job replied: "How you have helped the powerless! How you have saved the arm that is feeble! What advice you have offered to one without wisdom! And what great insight you have displayed! ... And these are but the outer fringe of his works; how faint the whisper we hear of him! Who then can understand the thunder of his power?"*

Dear Lord,

Fighting depression makes me feel powerless; I am without the wisdom to work through what troubles me. Thankfully, no matter how many times I repeat my feeble cry for help, you answer me with Your presence. I do not understand how, but You get me through breath by breath, until You give me the insight I need to go on.

# February

# 27

## PROVERBS
### 3:23–26

*Then you will go on your way in safety, and your foot will not stumble; when you lie down, you will not be afraid; when you lie down, your sleep will be sweet. Have no fear of sudden disaster or of the ruin that overtakes the wicked, for the Lord will be your confidence and will keep your foot from being snared.*

Dear Lord,

Worry and fear often steal my sleep at night; I need Your presence when I lay down to rest. Sudden disasters do overtake me, I do find myself in ruinous situations. I need to feel confident that You are still in control of my circumstances regardless of what I see around me; that You will keep me safe from wickedness and my feet from snares as I pass through the valleys of life. I am so blessed when I cry out to You in the night, and You give me rest and the strength to face tomorrow with hope beyond the valley of fear.

# February

# 28

## PROVERBS
## 12:14, 18, 25

Dear Lord,

Real and perceived life dramas often weigh me down with anxious thoughts. Thank you I may open my Bible and find kind words to lift me up. The power of Your Word is true and good—I pray You monitor the words from my mouth, that they will not be reckless, rather they are tempered with the fruit of Your Spirit to bring healing to the hurting because I have listened to Your wisdom and kept it in my heart.

*From the fruit of his lips a man is filled with good things as surely as the work of his hands reward him ... Reckless words pierce like a sword, but the tongue of the wise brings healing ... An anxious heart weighs a man down, but a kind word cheers him up.*

# February

# 29

## PROVERBS
13:12, 14:13, 15:13

*Hope deferred makes the heart sick, but a longing fulfilled is a tree of life ... Even in laughter the heart may ache, and joy may end in grief ... A happy heart makes the face cheerful, but heartache crushes the spirit.*

Dear Lord,

Through the years I have often thought that if only I were a stronger Christian, if only I had more faith and trust, I would not be devastated by heartache and grief. Thank you that Your Word has passages acknowledging logical human emotions in reaction to unfulfilled hopes, crushing heartaches. You know it makes me sick in spirit, even if I am laughing on the outside as if all were well, You know I am aching inside. Help me hold on to You when the longed for deliverance is delayed; turn my grief to quiet joy that You are my Deliverer, and it will come to pass in Your time.

# March

## 1

Dear Lord,

As I wage war against the negative influences that try to invade my home, I pray for Your wisdom and understanding to faithfully guide my children in Your direction. I deeply want our home built on Your love and strength. I ask that, through Your power, we hold and share the treasure of a close relationship with You and one another. May our rooms always be filled with Your comforting presence.

### PROVERBS 24:3–6

*By wisdom a house is built, and through understanding it is established; through knowledge its rooms are filled with rare and beautiful treasures. A wise man has great power, and a man of knowledge increases strength; for waging war you need guidance, and for victory many advisors.*

# March

# 2

## PROVERBS 27:1–2,21

*Do not boast about tomorrow, for you do not know what a day may bring forth. Let another praise you, and not your own mouth; someone else, and not your own lips ... The crucible for silver and the furnace for gold, but man is tested by the praise he receives.*

Dear Lord,

Low self-esteem is a constant foe of mine. I know I should not be full of self, yet do I not need some measure of self-confidence? Must I not limit my self-deprecation else I risk being an ineffective servant of Yours? Help me balance between acknowledging it is okay to have self respect, but draw the line at selfish pride. Not believing in myself limits my belief in You and what I can do through faith in Christ. May any praise I receive bring honor and recognition to You, and humble thankfulness to my heart for such blessings.

# March

# 3

## ECCLESIASTES
4:9–12

Dear Lord,

It's scriptures like this one that make my loneliness more pronounced—what if I do not have someone to help me work, help me get back up when I fall, to keep me warm, to help defend me in crisis? No one else to make a three strand cord? … thank you for reminding me You are my three strand cord: Father, Son and Holy Spirit. So though I am lonely, I am not alone. You are always with me. I always have You to help me.

*Two are better than one, because they have a good return for their work: If one falls down, his friend can help him up. But pity the man who falls and has no one to help him up! Also, if two lie down together, they will keep warm. But how can one keep warm alone? Though one may be overpowered, two can defend themselves. A cord of three strands is not quickly broken.*

# March

ISAIAH
30:15a, 18–19

*This is what the Sovereign Lord, the Holy One of Israel, says: "In repentance and rest is your salvation, in quietness and trust is your strength," ... Yet the Lord longs to be gracious to you; he rises to show you compassion. For the Lord is a God of justice. Blessed are all who wait for him! O people of Zion, who live in Jerusalem, you will weep no more. How gracious he will be when you cry for help! As soon as he hears, he will answer you.*

Dear Lord,

I cry for Your help. I repent of all my sins, I try to rest in confidence that You have my times in Your hands. Yet I struggle to maintain quietness of my spirit; I need Your strength. I need daily renewal of the assurance You hear my cries; I need daily answers to my concerns, even if it's just the quiet gracious response: "I am here." Thank you I can always trust You are here.

# March

# 5

Dear Lord,

Why does it sometimes feel like You disregard my suffering, suffering that is too much for me to bear and I need Your intervention quickly? I am weary, physically, emotionally and spiritually—there is no time in my hectic schedule to renew my strength. Why am I so weary? Is it because I have forgotten what I have heard, what I know to be true from Your Word? You are the Creator of the World, You are also my Creator, as insignificant as I am to the Universe. If only I ask, You will bring strength in place of my weakness—my hope is in You. Help me take those precious moments I need to be with You so You may calm my spirit, order my world, and give me courage to walk on because You are always near.

## ISAIAH 40:27–31

*Why do you say, O Jacob, and complain, O Israel, "My way is hidden from the Lord; my cause is disregarded by my God"? Do you not know? Have you not heard? The Lord is the everlasting God, the Creator of the ends of the earth. He will not grow tired or weary, and his understanding no one can fathom. He gives strength to the weary and increases the power of the weak. Even youths grow tired and weary, and young men stumble and fall; but those who hope in the Lord will renew their strength. They will soar on wings like eagles; they will run and not grow weary, they will walk and not faint.*

# March

# 6

### ISAIAH 46:3–4

*Listen to me, O house of Jacob, all you who remain of the house of Israel, you whom I have upheld since you were conceived, and have carried since your birth. Even to your old age and gray hairs I am he, I am he who will sustain you. I have made you and I will carry you; I will sustain you and I will rescue you.*

Dear Lord,

Help me believe Your promise— this promise that You will sustain me from birth to old age. Help me feel Your strength carry me through trouble times though I see no way I will be able to continue, yet know I must. I will persevere because You sustain me with Your mighty Spirit, reminding me You have made me especially for Your glory; You rescue me from despair and hopelessness.

# March

# 7

Dear Lord,

That is me! A wife deserted. I feel that not only did my husband reject me, but You abandoned me too—otherwise how could this have happened? Please, please, through Your deep compassion, bring back peace to my soul, bring back the knowledge that You have not, and will not, abandon me. I pray You will heal my broken spirit, comfort me with Your everlasting presence, continue molding me in Your image so I may be useful to You once again.

## ISAIAH 54:6–7

*"The Lord will call you back as if you were a wife deserted and distressed in spirit—a wife who married young, only to be rejected," says your God. "For a brief moment I abandoned you, but with deep compassion I will bring you back."*

# March 8

## ISAIAH 61:1–2A

*The Spirit of the Sovereign Lord is on me, because the Lord has anointed me to preach good news to the poor. He has sent me to bind up the brokenhearted, to proclaim freedom for the captives and release from darkness the prisoners, to proclaim the year of the Lord's favor and the day of vengeance of our God ...*

Dear Lord,

I pray You cause Your Spirit to move across my barren soul. I am the poor in spirit, I am the brokenhearted, I am the captive of fears, I am the forsaken prisoner, all within the darkness of my own despair. Shower Your favor upon me, let me see Your guiding light, proclaim to my soul I am free because of Your love, and I will make it through the despair to Your peace if only I hold on to You.

# March

## 9

### JEREMIAH
### 31:13B, 16–17, 18B–19

Dear Lord,

More than once I have made the wrong decision, and discovered it too late to avoid at least some of the consequences. I weep from regret, needing Your comfort to restore me. Please turn my mourning to gladness—help me work my way back into Your plan for my life. Then, I pray You reward me with peace and renewed fellowship with You.

*I will turn their mourning into gladness; I will give them comfort and joy instead of sorrow ... This is what the Lord says: "Restrain your voice from weeping and your eyes from tears, for your work will be rewarded," declares the Lord .... "So there is hope for your future," declares the Lord ... Restore me, and I will return, because you are the Lord my God. After I strayed, I repented: after I came to understand, I beat my breast. I was ashamed and humiliated because I bore the disgrace of my youth.*

# March

# 10

## MATTHEW
### 10:28–31

*Do not be afraid of those who kill the body but cannot kill the soul. Rather, be afraid of the One who can destroy both soul and body in hell. Are not two sparrows sold for a penny? Yet not one of them will fall to the ground apart from the will of your Father. And even the very hairs of your head are all numbered. So don't be afraid; you are worth more than many sparrows.*

Dear Lord,

I understand that I should try not to fear man and the physical harm that may happen in this world. The body can heal; if it does not a Christian's soul goes home to heaven. Spiritual damage, however, may be irreparable. Protect my faith, so difficulties do not turn me from You—loss of faith in the one true God is terminal for eternity. There is a whole continuum of spiritual healing and strength I need in this world. I am walking wounded Lord; please do not let difficulties destroy my usefulness to You.

# March

# 11

### LUKE
12:6–7

Dear Lord,

I am sorry, but I feel forgotten sometimes. I try and try, yet continue to struggle to feel worthwhile in this world. Though the world may see them as small and insignificant, You value even small sparrows. Help me to believe Your Word that you value me even more.

*Are not five sparrows sold for two pennies? Yet not one of them is forgotten by God. Indeed, the very hairs on your head are all numbered. Don't be afraid; you are worth more than many sparrows.*

# March

# 12

### LUKE 18:1–6

*Then Jesus told his disciples a parable to show them they should always pray and not give up. He said: "In a certain town there was a judge who neither feared God nor cared about men. And there was a widow who kept coming to him with the plea, 'Grant me justice against my adversary.' For some time he refused. But finally he said to himself, 'Even though I don't fear God or care about men, yet because this widow keeps bothering me, I will see she gets justice, so that she won't eventually wear me out with her coming!'" And the Lord said, "Listen to what the unjust judge says. And will not God bring about justice for his chosen ones, who cry out to him day and night?*

Dear Lord,

There are days I feel like giving up. I feel my heartfelt prayers do not reach Your ears. I do not understand Your silence. My pleas are not vain and/or foolish, but humble and sincere, in line with Your Word— yet You are silent … for years. Help me pray continually and not give up, but have faith and discernment that the answers will come in Your time.

# March

# 13

## ROMANS
5:3–5

Dear Lord,

I do not know that I can rejoice in my suffering; however, I need the rewards of perseverance. Thank you for the character qualities You develop in me as I move forward with Your guidance, ultimately getting past the excruciating pain. I then realize I can rejoice because my hope is in You. You cause me to overcome and succeed by pouring Your loving presence into my heart, with the assurance You will always be here for me. You never disappoint because You always show me the better way, and I reap the benefits after the suffering. Therefore, I can trust You with all my heart, soul and mind through both the sufferings and the blessings.

*Not only so, but we also rejoice in our sufferings, because we know that suffering produces perseverance; perseverance, character; and character, hope. And hope does not disappoint us, because God has poured out his love into our hearts by the Holy Spirit, whom he has given us.*

# March

# 14

## II CORINTHIANS
## 10:3–5

*For though we live in the world, we do not wage war as the world does. The weapons we fight with are not the weapons of the world. On the contrary, they have divine power to demolish strongholds. We demolish arguments and every pretension that sets itself up against the knowledge of God, and we take captive every thought to make it obedient to Christ.*

Dear Lord,

I struggle with worldly things—pain, disillusionment, depression, anxiousness, injustice, fear of the unknown. I lose sight of the divine power in spiritual weapons—Your Word, prayer, faith, obedience, salvation through the Cross. Help me take captive all my treacherous thoughts, comfort me in the knowledge and wisdom of Your Sovereignty. Demolish the worldly strongholds in my life, so I may be Your useful servant.

# March

# 15

Dear Lord,

This teaching is hard to comprehend; hard to accept the thorn in my flesh that has worn me down to nothing could be for my good. I have pleaded with you three times three thousand times to take it from me—yet it is still with me. The many years continue to pass and I continue experiencing devastating, painful torment. I continue to plead for Your merciful deliverance from ravaging effects of emotional, mental and physical agony. Though You have not delivered me in the way I have asked, I know Your powerful grace continues to sustain my spirit in my weakness. Then I realize, perhaps I comprehend this teaching after all.

## II CORINTHIANS 12:7–10

*To keep me from becoming conceited because of these surpassingly great revelations, there was given me a thorn in my flesh, a messenger of Satan, to torment me. Three times I pleaded with the Lord to take it away from me. But he said to me, "My grace is sufficient for you, for my power is made perfect in weakness." Therefore I will boast all the more gladly about my weaknesses, so that Christ's power may rest on me. That is why, for Christ's sake, I delight in weaknesses, in insults, in hardships, in persecutions, in difficulties. For when I am weak, then I am strong.*

# March

# 16

### PHILIPPIANS 4:6–7

*Do not be anxious about anything, but in everything, by prayer and petition, with thanksgiving, present your requests to God. And the peace of God, which transcends all understanding, will guard your hearts and your minds in Christ Jesus.*

Dear Lord,

Your Word says not to be anxious, yet this never-ending pain within goes deep down, cutting through my soul. Help me feel Your peace that passes understanding, bathe my soul in the healing waters of our mingled tears. Guard my mind and heart from despairing thoughts of helplessness, and resignation to irreparable loss of hope. You transcend the worldly pain and suffering, You raise my soul above it all in answer to my prayer. Humbly, I am so thankful for Your everlasting presence in my life.

# March

# 17

Dear Lord,

My thoughts are too often full of worry and hurt, too often full of fear and regret. I need to be reminded that though I have battles, I have more blessings. Thank you for Your 'whatever is' scripture, it purposefully directs my thoughts to positive things, to positive behaviors. I pray You make me an example of Your character, which is true, noble, right, pure, lovely, admirable; You are more than excellent and I devote my life to praising You.

### PHILIPPIANS 4:8–9

*Finally, brothers, whatever is true, whatever is noble, whatever is right, whatever is pure, whatever is lovely, whatever is admirable—if anything is excellent or praiseworthy—think about such things. Whatever you have learned or received or heard from me, or seen in me—put it into practice. And the God of peace will be with you.*

# March

# 18

## II TIMOTHY 1:12–14

*That is why I am suffering as I am. Yet I am not ashamed, because I know whom I have believed, and am convinced that he is able to guard what I have entrusted to him for that day. What you heard from me, keep as the pattern of sound teaching, with faith and love in Christ Jesus. Guard the good deposit that was entrusted to you—guard it with the help of the Holy Spirit who lives in us.*

Dear Lord,

Not all of us will be persecuted for our beliefs as the disciples were, or as Christians in other countries are today. Yet there are situations that may arise where a person may be prompted or tempted to feel ashamed about their belief in You— with the disciples I say do not be ashamed of the gospel of Jesus Christ. I know in whom I have believed, I know You are able to guard what I have entrusted to You—my eternal soul. You deposited the Good News within my heart; the Good News that salvation is found only through You, Jesus Christ, God's only Begotten Son. Your Holy Spirit gives me sound teaching as I continually seek You through prayer and Bible study; Your absolute truths are engraved upon my heart as I daily walk with You.

# March

# 19

Dear Lord,

When I am weary and worn, I consider what You went through to cleanse my soul from sin. I think about the opposition You faced for being kind and helpful, loving and giving, thoughtful of others' needs and healing their pain. From the beginning the religious leaders were jealous of Your popularity. The crowds loved what You could do for them, until they were easily swayed by deceitful propaganda and the sin that so easily entangles. Please help me run the race with perseverance. Please continue to be the author and perfecter of my faith so though I may grow weary, and before I lose heart, You renew my strength.

## HEBREWS 12:1–3

*Therefore, since we are surrounded by such a great cloud of witnesses, let us throw off everything that hinders and the sin that so easily entangles, and let us run with perseverance the race marked out for us. Let us fix our eyes on Jesus, the author and perfecter of our faith, who for the joy set before him endured the cross, scorning its shame, and set down at the right hand of the throne of God. Consider him who endured such opposition from sinful men, so that you will not grow weary and lose heart.*

# March

# 20

## JAMES 1:2–8

*Consider it pure joy, my brothers, whenever you face trials of many kinds, because you know that the testing of your faith develops perseverance. Perseverance must finish its work so that you may be mature and complete, not lacking anything. If any of you lacks wisdom, he should ask God, who gives generously to all without finding fault, and it will be given to him. But when he asks, he must believe and not doubt, because he who doubts is like a wave of the sea, blown and tossed by the wind. That man should not think he will receive anything from the Lord; he is a double-minded man, unstable in all he does.*

Dear Lord,

Facing trials can be such a daunting task, especially several at a time, or ones that seem to go on and on, with no end in sight. How can I possibly count it as joy? I suffer doubts, I am tossed about as if on stormy waves; I am unstable. Is it really possible for lowly me to receive help from the Almighty God? Your Word tells me, because I have faith in You, I will be tested and tried; I need to persevere by gaining Your Wisdom and make it through. Then I do have joy through the trials-because You are the Rock of my salvation.

# March

# 21

## JAMES 1:12–18

Dear Lord,

It seems once I persevere through one trial, yet another, perhaps even more fierce, is upon me. I wonder if it is You tempting me, or allowing me to be tempted. Thank you for Your Word that reminds me not to be pulled into the shifting shadows of deceit, or dragged away from Your Truth. Your Word reminds me to stand firm in the test so that my faith continues to grow. You have promised me eternal life through faith in Jesus Christ, and once I am with You in Eternity, my trials will be forgotten in Your peaceful presence.

*Blessed is the man who perseveres under trial, because when he has stood the test, he will receive the crown of life that God has promised to those who love him. When tempted, no one should say, "God is tempting me." For God cannot be tempted by evil, nor does he tempt anyone; but each one is tempted when, by his own evil desire, he is dragged away and enticed. Then, after desire has conceived, it gives birth to sin; and sin, when it is full grown, gives birth to death. Don't be deceived, my dear brothers. Every good and perfect gift is from above, coming down from the Father of heavenly lights, who does not change like shifting shadows. He chose to give us birth through the word of truth that we might be a kind of first fruits of all he created.*

# March

# 22

### JAMES 5:11

*As you know, we consider blessed those who have persevered. You have heard of Job's perseverance and have seen what the Lord finally brought about. The Lord is full of compassion and mercy.*

Dear Lord,

Help me persevere through this difficult time. I know I need to continue against all odds, but my strength is more than gone. And it is hard to believe in the blessing when my heart is broken to the bone. As Job did, however, let me also feel Your presence in my soul, comforting me in the knowledge You will bring deliverance in Your time.

# March

# 23

Dear Lord,

Thank you that I may bring all my needs before you: when I am in trouble, when I am sick, and most importantly, when I need my sins washed away with Your precious cleansing blood. I pray You grant me faith where I am weak so I may grow stronger in Your love. Let me remember to praise You for the blessings You place in my life, both large and small. Make me effective for You.

## JAMES 5:13–16

*Is any one of you in trouble? He should pray. Is anyone happy? Let him sing songs of praise. Is anyone of you sick? He should call the elders of the church to pray over him and anoint him with oil in the name of the Lord. And the prayer offered in faith will make the sick person well; the Lord will raise him up. If he has sinned, he will be forgiven. Therefore confess your sins to each other and pray for each other so that you may be healed. The prayer of a righteous man is powerful and effective.*

# March

# 24

## 1 PETER 1:3–6

*Praise be to the God and Father of our Lord Jesus Christ! In his great mercy he has given us new birth into a living hope through the resurrection of Jesus Christ from the dead, and into an inheritance that can never perish, spoil or fade—kept in heaven for you, who through faith are shielded by God's power until the coming of the salvation that is ready to be revealed in the last time. In this you greatly rejoice, though now for a little while you may have had to suffer grief in all kinds of trials.*

Dear Lord,

Thank you for Your Word, with its reminders that though I may suffer grief and all kinds of trials, my inheritance is in heaven because I have faith in You, Jesus Christ, my Savior. The difficulties I face in this world cannot diminish nor spoil Your promises; they are eternal. Your power shields my soul from being destroyed; Your constant presence grows my faith; I will praise You all my days for great is Your mercy.

# March

# 25

Dear Lord,

I question why, why must there be trials and tribulations one after another until I am weary to the bone. Then Your Word answers me: so that my faith, which is more valuable than worldly riches, is genuine. There is no question—I want to be genuine. I have genuine faith in You, Lord, I feel Your presence in every aspect of my life, every moment of my life, though I cannot see You with my physical eyes. I want others to see You glorified in my life, whether they are believers or not, that they will know You are at home in my heart. Please give me strength to persevere in the trials as my faith and belief and praise remain steadfast.

## I PETER 1:7–9

*These [trials] have come so that your faith—of greater worth than gold, which perishes even though refined by fire— may be proved genuine and may result in praise, glory and honor when Jesus Christ is revealed. Though you have not seen him, you love him; and even though you do not see him now, you believe in him and are filled with an inexpressible and glorious joy, for you are receiving the goal of your faith, the salvation of your souls.*

# March

# 26

## 1 PETER 2:9–10

*But you are a chosen people, a royal priesthood, a holy nation, a people belonging to God, that you may declare the praises of him who called you out of darkness into his wonderful light. Once you were not a people, but now you are the people of God; once you had not received mercy, but now you have received mercy.*

Dear Lord,

Thank you for telling me I am chosen. You know my life -from conception to returning to dust. You know how 'un'-chosen I have felt most of my life. Your loving Presence sustains me. In a crowded room when I may feel the most alone, You remind me I belong to You—You disperse my darkness with Your merciful light. I am humbled that the One True Holy God takes time to comfort my broken soul when I am grieving lost dreams, fearing future disappointments, feeling responsible for all things all by myself. But I am only responsible to choose You as my Savior and follow Your guidance through the trials and blessings, praising You with all joy as I trust my life into Your merciful Hands.

# March

# 27

Dear Lord,

I am thankful that sometimes You deliver me from consequences and other times You allow me to learn from them. However, I do not understand when it seems I have done what is right, yet I am dragged into consequences caused by another's design. Your Word says I need to bear up under the unjust suffering to be an example. This is a hard teaching; I want, I need justice. I pray, though, when I suffer consequences from my own or another's actions, may it be to Your glory and honor. It is not for me to exact justice, only to be conscious that You are the Judge who will make all things right in the end. I praise the manifestations of Your love in my life.

## I PETER 2:19–21

*For it is commendable if a man bears up under the pain of unjust suffering because he is conscious of God. But how is it to your credit if you receive a beating for doing wrong and endure it? But if you suffer for doing good and you endure it, this is commendable before God. To this you were called, because Christ suffered for you, leaving you an example, that you should follow in his steps.*

# March

# 28

## 1 PETER 4:12–15

*Dear friends, do not be surprised at the painful trial you are suffering, as though something strange were happening to you. But rejoice that you participate in the suffering of Christ, so that you may be overjoyed when his glory is revealed. If you are insulted because of the name of Christ, you are blessed, for the Spirit of glory and of God rests on you. If you suffer, it should not be as a murderer or thief or any other kind of criminal, or even as a meddler.*

Dear Lord,

I serve You faithfully; I pray for protection, I do everything I think I am supposed to do, yet I still end up in a painful trial. Thank you for the reminder that suffering will happen—my Savior suffered, why would I not follow in His footsteps? The world mistreated, disrespected Him—I must expect the same in certain circumstances. I sincerely pray You keep me from willful sins for which it would be no surprise to suffer painful consequences. When I seem to suffer senselessly, remind me of this Scripture where You tell me, do not be surprised, it is for Your glory.

# March

# 29

## 1 PETER 5:8–11

Dear Lord,

Please help me to be self-controlled, steadfast in my pursuit of You, despite my sufferings. Sometimes they are from not being alert enough to avoid the stumbling blocks the devil has laid in my path, other times it's the very firm faith I have in You that incites the roar of the enemy. I pray for Your power to restore me over and over again, until I am safe with You in the peace and glory of heaven.

*Be self-controlled and alert. Your enemy the devil prowls around like a roaring lion looking for someone to devour. Resist him, standing firm in the faith, because you know that your brothers throughout the world are undergoing the same kind of sufferings. And the God of all grace, who called you to his eternal glory in Christ, after you have suffered a little while, will himself restore you and make you strong, firm and steadfast. To him be the power forever and ever. Amen.*

# March

# 30

## JUDE 22–25

*Be merciful to those who doubt; snatch others from the fire and save them; to others show mercy, mixed with fear—hating even the clothing stained by corrupted flesh. To him who is able to keep you from falling and to present you before his glorious presence without fault and with great joy—to the only God our Savior be glory, majesty, power and authority, through Jesus Christ our Lord, before all ages, now and forevermore! Amen.*

Dear Lord,

Thank you for Your mercy and grace that snatched me from the fire of sin, which burns a soul to ashes. Because Your love delivered me and Your presence leads me in the way I should go, I will forever praise You, the Father, the Son and the Holy Ghost. You were, You are, You will always be the Sovereign King of all the ages, over all Your creation. All power and authority belong to You—nothing happens to me without Your knowledge. Hear my sincere prayers for mercy and victory; You keep me from falling in ways I do not even know. I will bow with joy and thanksgiving at Your throne, to worship You eternally.

# March

# 31

Dear Lord,

How is it I am lost from the fold before I realize what happened? That I have somehow forgotten Your rightful place is on the throne of my heart and life every day in every way? Help me always look to You, my Shepherd, to lead me in the right direction. And when I stray, thank you from the bottom of my broken heart that You lead me back, drying my tears of regret and sorrow—and the ones of joy for being restored to fellowship with my Savior.

## REVELATIONS 7:17

*For the Lamb at the center of the throne will be their shepherd; he will lead them to springs of living water. And God will wipe away every tear from their eyes.*

100

# Bread of Life

# April

# 1

Dear Lord,

When I try to comprehend the vastness of the heavens, I am struck anew with how miniscule my existence is in the cosmos. How is it You bear in mind what happens to me? How is it You care about me personally and individually amongst all Creation? I do not understand the how and why—I am just so grateful for feeling Your Spirit within me assuring me it is so. Thank You!

## PSALM 8: 3–4

*When I consider your heavens, the work of your fingers, the moon and the stars, which you have set in place, what is man that you are mindful of him, the son of man that you care for him?*

# April 2

## PSALM 16:1–2, 5–6

*Keep me safe, O God, for in you I take refuge. I said to the Lord, "You are my Lord; apart from you I have no good thing ..." Lord, you have assigned me my portion and my cup; you have made my lot secure. The boundary lines have fallen for me in pleasant places; surely I have a delightful inheritance.*

Dear Lord,

It is true—apart from You I have no good thing. If I were the richest or the poorest, the most fair or the most foul, at peace or in turmoil, I have nothing if I do not have You dwelling within. I grumble because of my lot in life; however You are my portion and I am spiritually safe because of Your salvation, therefore I should always rejoice because of the eternal inheritance I have through Jesus Christ. Surely my cup runneth over with Your love and blessings.

# April

## 3

Dear Lord,

How can I foresee when my good intentions turn awry and become willful disobedience to Your Word? Help me so that the hurts I bear do not override my desire to do Your will, that I do not seek out inappropriate balm for my pain, but always bring it before You for the supernatural healing treatment.

### PSALM 19:12–14

*Who can discern his errors? Forgive my hidden faults. Keep your servant also from willful sins; may they not rule over me. Then will I be blameless, innocent of great transgression. May the words of my mouth and the meditation of my heart be pleasing in your sight, O Lord, my Rock and my Redeemer.*

# April

PSALM 20:1–5

*May the Lord answer you when you are in distress; may the name of the God of Jacob protect you. May he send you help from the sanctuary and grant you support from Zion. May he remember all your sacrifices and accept your burnt offerings. May he give you the desire of your heart and make all your plans succeed. We will shout for joy when you are victorious and will lift up our banners in the name of our God. May the Lord grant all your requests.*

Dear Lord,

I pray you will answer me in my distress—You know the desires of my heart. You know I hope for things within Your will, not in opposition to Your Word. Please grant my request for healing and strength that my heart will remain strong for You to use according to Your plan. As I wait within Your sanctuary, I know I have victory through the Lord my God.

# April

# 5

Dear Lord,

I honestly want to know Your ways, understand Your truths, follow all Your teachings. Forgive, I pray, my sins and rebellious ways; guide me along obedient and peaceful paths. You are good and loving—help others see You in me as I live in Your protective shadow all the days of my life.

PSALM 25:4–7

*Show me your ways, O Lord, teach me your paths; guide me in your truth and teach me, for you are God my Savior, and my hope is in you all day long. Remember, O Lord, your great mercy and love, for they are from of old. Remember not the sins of my youth and my rebellious ways; according to your love remember me, for you are good, O Lord.*

# April

# 6

### PSALM 25:8–12

*Good and upright is the Lord; therefore he instructs sinners in his ways. He guides the humble in what is right and teaches them his way. All the ways of the Lord are loving and faithful for those who keep the demands of his covenant. For the sake of your name, O Lord, forgive my iniquity, though it is great. Who, then, is the man that fears the Lord? He will instruct him in the way chosen for him.*

Dear Lord,

I humbly ask for Your instruction. Mankind is destined to err—thank you for Your covenant of love, Your forgiveness of sin, Your faithful ways. Instruct me down the path You have chosen for me. When I stray off to another of my own choosing, I pray for Your forgiveness and mercy to bring me back into obediently following, both when the path is smooth and when it is rough.

# April 7

Dear Lord,

When I am in the day of trouble, remind me to gaze upon Your beauty; Your beauty living in the nature around me, in those I love, in the comfort of Your Word, in Your presence in my heart. You dwell within my soul; I pray You build in me Your spiritual temple where I may draw within the hidden shelter, secure that I am anchored to the Solid Rock.

## PSALM 27:4–5

*One thing I ask of the Lord, this is what I seek: that I may dwell in the house of the Lord all the days of my life, to gaze upon the beauty of the Lord and to seek him in his temple. For in the day of trouble he will keep me safe in his dwelling; he will hide me in the shelter of his tabernacle and set me high upon a rock.*

# April

# 8

### PSALM 31:7–8, 14–16

*I will be glad and rejoice in your love, for you saw my affliction and knew the anguish of my soul. You have not handed me over to the enemy but have set my feet in a spacious place. .. But I trust in you, O Lord; I say, "You are my God." My times are in your hands; deliver me from my enemies and from those who pursue me. Let your face shine on your servant; save me in your unfailing love.*

Dear Lord,

You are the only one who sees my afflictions, who knows the depth of my soul's anguish. Yet even in these depths, I know You are my God, my times are in Your Hands. I must trust in You for deliverance from my enemy, whether it be depression, pain, loneliness, failure, or fear of the unknown. Please know I am sincerely Your servant, and humbly appreciate Your unfailing love that pursues my spirit to assure my steps are ordered by Your grand design.

# April

# 9

Dear Lord,

How many times have I cried out in alarm 'I am cut off from your sight!' How many times have I felt like a besieged city about to fall? And how many times have You heard my cry, and mercifully provided me with your strength each and every time. It's more times than I can count, yet here I am again asking You to please continue strengthening me, whether I am besieged by responsibilities, by circumstances, by the unknown. Remind me my hope is in You, the Preserver of my soul, who daily shows His wonderful love to me.

PSALM 31:21–24

*Praise be to the Lord, for he showed his wonderful love to me when I was a besieged city. In my alarm I said, "I am cut off from your sight!" Yet you heard my cry for mercy when I called to you for help. Love the Lord, all his saints! The Lord preserves the faithful, but the proud he pays back in full. Be strong and take heart, all you who hope in the Lord.*

# April

# 10

## PSALM 32:1–5

*Blessed is he whose transgressions are forgiven, whose sins are covered. Blessed is the man whose sin the Lord does not count against him and in whose spirit is no deceit. When I kept silent, my bones wasted away through my groaning all day long. For day and night your hand was heavy upon me; my strength was sapped as in the heat of summer. Then I acknowledged my sin to you and did not cover up my iniquity. I said, "I will confess my transgressions to the Lord"—and you forgave the guilt of my sin.*

Dear Lord,

I invariably have times of failure. I cannot let my spirit remain silent; I must acknowledge my sins, all my weaknesses, otherwise my soul wastes away and I feel You are far from me. I confess my transgressions to You, deeply thankful for Your forgiveness and the freedom from guilt it brings. You remind me You are never far away; You are always as close as the mention of Your Name. Thank you Lord.

# April

# 11

Dear Lord,

Be my hiding place—the safe haven where I may run and hide, shedding my tears in private because You alone are able to comfort and deliver me from this excruciating heartache. Counsel me how to move on from here; teach me the way I should go so that I know, that I know, that I know my world is in Your control, not controlled by the woes of this world. I will forever sing in worship of Your unfailing love.

## PSALM 32:7–11

*You are my hiding place; you will protect me from trouble and surround me with songs of deliverance. I will instruct you and teach you in the way you should go; I will counsel you and watch over you. Do not be like the horse or the mule, which have no understanding but must be controlled by bit and bridle or they will not come to you. Many are the woes of the wicked, but the Lord's unfailing love surrounds the man who trusts in him. Rejoice in the Lord and be glad, you righteous; sing, all you who are upright in heart!*

# April

# 12

### PSALM 33:4–11

*For the word of the Lord is right and true; he is faithful in all he does. The Lord loves righteousness and justice; the earth is full of his unfailing love. By the word of the Lord were the heavens made, their starry host by the breath of his mouth. He gathers the waters of the sea into jars; he puts the deep into storehouses. Let all the earth fear the Lord; let all the people of the world revere him. For he spoke, and it came to be; he commanded, and it stood firm. The Lord foils the plans of the nations; he thwarts the purposes of the peoples. But the plans of the Lord stand firm forever, the purposes of his heart through all generations.*

Dear Lord,

It is hard to believe that the Creator of the Universe, the Supreme Being who spoke and all there is came into being, has plans for infinitesimally small me. Yet I undoubtedly know Your Word is right and true, and You have purposes for all generations until Your return. Even as it seems fewer and fewer people in the world revere You, still will I praise Your righteousness and justice. Thank you for Your faithfulness and that You have plans for me, firm plans that go on forever.

# April

# 13

Dear Lord,

Your love is priceless, and free to both the high and low; those times when I feel high with needs and low in spirit. When the heat of battle is too much, I need Your soothing fountain of life to refresh me, Your continuous light to draw me forward along the path of righteousness. Thank you for guiding my heart in the direction of my eternal refuge as I seek to know You better and better each day.

## PSALM 36:7–10

*How priceless is your unfailing love! Both high and low among men find refuge in the shadow of your wings. They feast on the abundance of your house; you give them drink from your river of delights. For with you is the fountain of life; in your light we see light. Continue your love to those who know you, your righteousness to the upright in heart.*

# April

# 14

## PSALM 37:39–40

*The salvation of the righteous comes from the Lord; he is their stronghold in time of trouble. The Lord helps them and delivers them; he delivers them from the wicked and saves them, because they take refuge in him.*

Dear Lord,

Thank you for my spiritual salvation through faith in Jesus Christ. You are my righteousness, my stronghold, my refuge. I need You not only for my spiritual salvation, but also for the emotional, physical and financial. I deeply need You to deliver me from inner troubles, real and imagined, that only You can see and understand. Be my stronghold from those hurts and fears that assail my heart daily. They often would overwhelm my spirit if not for Your sustaining presence in my soul. I know you are my deliverance.

# April

# 15

Dear Lord,

Thank you for defining right and wrong, and giving me the knowledge to know the difference. Thank you for the knowledge of who You are, the Almighty God who created the heavens and the earth, God the Father, Son and Holy Spirit. Thank you for my conscience, the conviction of the Holy Spirit when I have done wrong. When I have transgressed against Your law, remind me the laws are for my protection, not to punish me. You are the true and righteous Judge; thank you I may plead the covering of the blood of Jesus and be cleansed from sin through His sacrifice and Your great compassion.

## PSALM 51:1–4

*Have mercy on me, O God, according to your unfailing love; according to your great compassion blot out my transgressions. Wash away all my iniquity and cleanse me from my sin. For I know my transgressions, and my sin is always before me. Against you, you only, have I sinned and done what is evil in your sight, so that you are proved right when you speak and justified when you judge.*

# April

# 16

## PSALM 51:5–9

*Surely I was sinful at birth, sinful from the time my mother conceived me. Surely you desire truth in the inner parts; you teach me wisdom in the inmost place. Cleanse me with hyssop, and I will be clean; wash me, and I will be whiter than snow. Let me hear joy and gladness; let the bones you have crushed rejoice. Hide your face from my sins and blot out all my iniquity.*

Dear Lord,

I commit sins even though I have Your truths written on my heart. Each time I fail, I feel useless to You and hopeless in my quest to serve You faithfully. But You knew from the beginning I would struggle; in Your great mercy you sent Jesus to live and die and rise again to cover my sin when I ask forgiveness. You teach me wisdom, cleanse my soul from sin, and with a humble, joyful heart I endeavor to serve You better each day with all my heart, soul and mind.

# April

# 17

Dear Lord,

Sometimes it seems so hard to follow Your Way, and I fail. I pray You do not cast me aside, giving up on me because I have once again come forward with a broken, contrite heart that needs to be cleansed and healed through Your holy forgiveness. Thank You that You do not despise my broken spirit, rather You will heal it in Your tender mercy. Create in me a pure heart after every failure and forgiveness; make me more steadfast in my quest to follow Your Word. I pray for a more willing spirit, I pray the joy of Your salvation will continue to sustain me.

## PSALM 51:10–12, 17

*Create in me a pure heart, O God, and renew a steadfast spirit within me. Do not cast me from your presence or take your Holy Spirit from me. Restore to me the joy of your salvation and grant me a willing spirit, to sustain me ... The sacrifices of God are a broken spirit; a broken and contrite heart, O God, you will not despise.*

# April

# 18

## PSALM 62:5–8

*Find rest, O my soul, in God alone; my hope comes from him. He alone is my rock and my salvation; he is my fortress, I will not be shaken. My salvation and my honor depend on God; he is my mighty rock, my refuge. Trust in him at all times, O people; pour out your hearts to him, for God is our refuge.*

Dear Lord,

My soul badly needs Your rest; I sincerely pour out my heart to You, knowing You are my refuge. Sometimes I feel so alone, so shaken, that I cannot feel Your presence. Yet my hope is still in You—stop my fearful heart from shaking, from staring helplessly at the coming onslaught of the enemy. Rather let me see Your fortress of love is round about me. Let my attitude faithfully honor You while in crisis, as I trust in You alone for deliverance.

# April
# 19

## PSALM 63:1–4, 6–8

*O God, you are my God, earnestly I seek you; my soul thirsts for you, my body longs for you, in a dry and weary land where there is no water. I have seen you in the sanctuary and beheld your power and your glory. Because your love is better than life, my lips will glorify you. I will praise you as long as I live, and in your name I will lift up my hands … On my bed I remember you; I think of you through the watches of the night. Because you are my help, I sing in the shadow of your wings. My soul clings to you; your right hand upholds me.*

Dear Lord,

There are days I feel like a prisoner abandoned in the desert with no food or water, and there seems no way out. Yet I have seen Your power work in my life time after time when I thought there was no way I could make it through. I earnestly seek Your presence at night, often while lying awake in physical pain and emotional darkness. With my hands lifted up, my soul strains to reach the inner sanctuary where You live. Then You gently, soothingly remind me my heart is Your dwelling place. Once again my soul is quieted by the knowledge You hold my life in Your right hand. You are watching over me always.

# April

# 20

## PSALM 73:21–26

*When my heart was grieved and my spirit embittered, I was senseless and ignorant; I was a brute beast before you. Yet I am always with you; you hold me by my right hand. You guide me with your counsel, and afterward you will take me into glory. Whom have I in heaven but you? And earth has nothing I desire besides you. My flesh and my heart may fail, but God is the strength of my heart and my portion forever.*

Dear Lord,

My heart grieves, and in my grief sometimes my spirit becomes embittered. I struggle to understand Your counsel when I am suffering such heartache. My flesh and my heart fail; it is such a comfort that You are always with me, even when I doubt. In those times, I pray for Your strength to overcome the bitterness, to overcome the grief, and to triumph by learning the life lesson in the suffering. May You always guide me; You are my portion in this life and the one to come. Keep me from being ignorant of Your ways. Through unshakable faith I have the blessed assurance You are my Savior- and ultimately that is all I ever need.

# April

# 21

## PSALM 85:2–9

*You forgave the iniquity of your people and covered all their sins. You set aside all your wrath and turned from your fierce anger. Restore us again, O God our Savior, and put away your displeasure toward us. Will you be angry with us forever? Will you prolong your anger through all generations? Will you not revive us again, that your people may rejoice in you? Show us your unfailing love, O Lord, and grant us your salvation. I will listen to what God the Lord will say; he promises peace to his people, his saints—but let them not return to folly. Surely his salvation is near those who fear him, that his glory may dwell in our land.*

Dear Lord,

I so need Your unfailing love, Your salvation, Your peace, Your glory to dwell within my soul. I listen to Your Word, I feel Your presence, I fear how infinitely great You are, and know how infinitesimally insignificant I am. I fear that when I fail, when I return to my folly despite my sincere love for You, You will no longer consider me one of Your people. I pray sincerely, humbly for Your unfailing love to once again cover my sins with the blood of the Lamb. Draw me near, reviving my spirit with Your peace that passes understanding. I wait before You, listening for Your instructions for my life; it is my heart's desire to bring glory to my God and Savior.

# April

# 22

## PSALM 86:5–8, 11–13

*You are forgiving and good, O Lord, abounding in love to all who call to you. Hear my prayer, O Lord; listen to my cry for mercy. In the day of my trouble I will call to you, for you will answer me. Among the gods there is none like you, O Lord; no deeds can compare with yours ... Teach me your way, O Lord, and I will walk in your truth; give me an undivided heart, that I may fear your name. I will praise you, O Lord my God, with all my heart; I will glorify your name forever. For great is your love toward me; you have delivered me from the depths of the grave.*

Dear Lord,

O, that You would grant me an undivided heart that I would never let You down again! My spirit is unwaveringly determined to follow Your way; my flesh is too imperfect and too troubled, causing my attention to be divided from my spirit's desires. I cry to You for reconciliation; thanking You that as You teach me Your way, walking in Your truth continues to close that great divide. There is no god like You; all others are man-made, they can do nothing, it is pointless to compare them to You. Only Your Name is worthy of praise and honor. Thank you for answering my prayer for merciful forgiveness, abiding patience and Your great love. Your goodness constantly draws me nearer to thee, my Creator and Savior.

# April

# 23

Dear Lord,

I pray You see my spirit sincerely bow to You, recognizing Your Majesty over the Universe. You alone are worthy of worship. You spoke Creation into being, we are created by the work of Your Hands. Despite our imperfections and outright rebellion, You keep us under Your care. Thank you for the gift of music and song You give to others so they may lead us in worship and praise to You, with words I would not have known to express. You are the King of kings, Lord of lords, there is no God besides You. You are the Rock I cling to in trials, and upon which I stand in victory over tribulation.

## PSALM 95:1–7

*Come, let us sing for joy to the Lord; let us shout aloud to the Rock of our salvation. Let us come before him with thanksgiving and extol him with music and song. For the Lord is the great God, the great King above all gods. In his hand are the depths of the earth, and the mountain peaks belong to him. The sea is his, for he made it, and his hands formed the dry land. Come, let us bow down in worship, let us kneel before the Lord our Maker; for he is our God and we are the people of his pasture, the flock under his care.*

# April

# 24

### PSALM 103:1–5, 10–12

*Praise the Lord, O my soul; all my inmost being, praise his holy name. Praise the Lord, O my soul, and forget not all his benefits—who forgives all your sins and heals all your diseases, who redeems your life from the pit and crowns you with love and compassion, who satisfies your desires with good things so that your youth is renewed like the eagle's … he does not treat us as our sins deserve or repay us according to our iniquities. For as high as the heavens are above the earth, so great is his love for those who fear him; as far as the east is from the west, so far has he removed our transgressions from us.*

Dear Lord,

From my inmost being, from the deepest part of my soul that only You know, I thank you for being with me always. For forgiving me, for continually healing my hurts, for repeatedly rescuing me from the pit of despair. While life is complex, and sin abounds, You renew my heavy heart when it is burdened by sin and sorrow; Your forgiveness and forgetfulness of the sin that has come before gives me strength once again to rise above all that entangles my good intentions. With loving compassion, You use me for Your good purposes. You raise my spirit up into the heavens with You, reminding me I am simply on a journey to my eternal home.

# April

## 25

Dear Lord,

How many times, like the psalmist, have I felt pushed back and about to fall! The battle ahead is just too much, my strength is gone. But if I close my eyes, take a moment to seek Your face, a worship hymn will wash peace over my soul. Sometimes it is a shout of victory, more often times it is a gentle, thankful sigh of relief that once again I made it through the darkness by the light of my Savior's love. The humble joy I feel for my salvation through Jesus Christ's sacrifice, who has and will always sit at the right hand of Your throne, reminds me victory is mine through faith and trust in You. Surely You have done great things in me!

### PSALM 118:13–16

*I was pushed back and about to fall, but the Lord helped me. The Lord is my strength and my song; he has become my salvation. Shouts of joy and victory resound in the tents of the righteous: "The Lord's right hand has done mighty things! The Lord's right hand is lifted high; the Lord's right hand has done mighty things!"*

# April

# 26

## PSALM 118:22–29

*The stone the builders rejected has become the capstone; the Lord has done this, and it is marvelous in our eyes. This is the day the Lord has made; let us rejoice and be glad in it. O Lord save us; O Lord, grant us success. Blessed is he who comes in the name of the Lord. From the house of the Lord we bless you. The Lord is God, and he has made his light shine upon us. With boughs in hand, join in the festal procession up to the horns of the alter. You are my God, and I will give you thanks; you are my God, and I will exalt you. Give thanks to the Lord, for he is good; his love endures forever.*

Dear Lord,

Some days it is hard to find a reason for joy, a reason to smile. Thank you for Your Word reminding me You made this day and there is always a reason to rejoice. You are the Savior of the world—Your love endures forever. Every day You love me, care for me, guide me; for this I praise and worship You, and in that I am glad every day. Thank you for saving me, thank you for the successes You give me, thank you for the failures You bring me through so I may be stronger and wiser than before. You are the cornerstone of my foundation; I am humbled by Your marvelous works in my behalf. May my life glorify Your Name.

# April
# 27

Dear Lord,

I have set my heart on Your laws, knowing they are for my good; knowing when I break them, You have provided forgiveness and redemption for me when I have sincere regret for my transgression. When the world's troubles weigh my spirit down with sorrow, I pray You strengthen me through Your Word. Be gracious and let me understand and grow through the troubles. I hold fast to You, Lord, through faith. Only in You am I free from the world's weariness; only You can provide peace for my soul.

## PSALM 119:27–32

*Let me understand the teaching of your precepts; then I will meditate on your wonders. My soul is weary with sorrow; strengthen me according to your word. Keep me from deceitful ways; be gracious to me through your law. I have chosen the way of truth; I have set my heart on your laws. I hold fast to your statutes, O Lord; do not let me be put to shame. I run in the path of your commands, for you have set my heart free.*

# April

# 28

## PSALM 119:65–68, 71

*Do good to your servant according to your word, O Lord. Teach me knowledge and good judgment, for I believe in your commands. Before I was afflicted I went astray, but now I obey your word. You are good, and what you do is good; teach me your decrees ... It was good for me to be afflicted so I might learn your decrees.*

Dear Lord,

Though I pursue knowledge to continually grow and learn as an individual, without good judgment the knowledge will not be tempered into wisdom. Teach me to obey your decrees and not be led astray by worldly knowledge. Help me understand that sometimes a good servant must be allowed to suffer physical, emotional, spiritual afflictions in order to learn good judgment and the value of Your decrees. I pray to believe and obey them all the days of my life.

# April

# 29

Dear Lord,

I am so tired of weeping, so tired of feeling the load I carry is too much for me. I need You to sow the seeds of persistence, endurance, long suffering in my soul, along with the confidence that they will grow to bring my soul victory as each challenge is met and conquered with You guiding my way. I pray Your harvest from my soul will be joyful, and a blessing to You and those around me. As I worship You, often in song, I feel Your Presence, and I am reminded that having You in my heart, soul and mind, if no other blessing is ever given, will always fill me with great spiritual joy. Surely You have done great things in my life.

## PSALM 126:3–6

*The Lord has done great things for us, and we are filled with joy. Restore our fortunes, O Lord, like streams in the Negev. Those who sow in tears will reap with songs of joy. He who goes out weeping, carrying seed to sow, will return with songs of joy, carrying sheaves with him.*

# April

# 30

## PSALM 138:3, 6–8

*When I called, you answered me; you made me bold and stouthearted ... Though the Lord is on high, he looks upon the lowly, but the proud he knows from afar. Though I walk in the midst of trouble, you preserve my life; you stretch out your hand against the anger of my foes, with your right hand you save me. The Lord will fulfill his purpose for me; your love, O Lord, endures forever—do not abandon the works of your hands.*

Dear Lord,

I believe You are my Creator and Savior; please do not abandon working in me, though I so often fail to follow Your lead. Thank You for hearing my call for mercy in the midst of my trouble, saving me from my foes within and without. I believe You will fulfill Your purpose for my life, even when my willful disobedience or inadvertent ignorance gets in the way. I pray for a bold and resolute heart to live for You so others may see and believe Your love endures forever.

# May

# 1

Dear Lord,

You know me as no other. You see behind the mask I wear for all the others to see. You know the emotional struggles I have when I go out amongst the others. You know the haunting hurts that trouble my soul when I lay down to sleep. And You are familiar with the simple things that make me smile. I pray You guide my tongue when I speak that my speech will be pleasing to You. Thank you for being mindful of me, at my best and at my worst. Surround me with Your presence that I may know Your hand is always upon my life.

### PSALM 139:1–6

*O Lord, you have searched me and you know me. You know when I sit and when I rise; you perceive my thoughts from afar. You discern my going out and my lying down; you are familiar with all my ways. Before a word is on my tongue you know it completely, O Lord. You hem me in—behind and before; you have laid your hand upon me. Such knowledge is too wonderful for me, too lofty for me to attain.*

# May

# 2

### PSALM 139:13–14

*For you created my inmost being; you knit me together in my mother's womb. I praise you because I am fearfully and wonderfully made; your works are wonderful, I know that full well.*

Dear Lord,

Please remind me to read this Psalm when I am feeling insignificant, worthless, of no consequence. The Creator of the Universe Himself knit me together in my mother's womb. You created my inmost being, the person who I am deep in my spirit known only to You. You know me personally, as an individual, better than I know myself. You have planned the works You will perform in my life for Your glory. Knowing You created me with a purpose, no matter what I think or feel, I am a significant and remarkable being because I belong to You. May I humbly serve the purpose for which You made me.

# May

## 3

Dear Lord,

My burdens keep me bowed down, I repeatedly need You to lift me up. I am sorry for my weakness, and ever grateful for Your boundless compassion and love. You faithfully keep Your promises to me, slow to anger when I fail you, quick to re-direct me to Your path of success. I worship You for Your goodness. May my life be a living testament honoring Your kingdom. May others see the mighty acts You have done in my life; may I give You the praise and glory that is Your due. Your truth stands through all generations.

### PSALM 145:8–14

*The Lord is gracious and compassionate, slow to anger and rich in love. The Lord is good to all; he has compassion on all he has made. All you have made will praise you, O Lord; your saints will extol you. They will tell of the glory of your kingdom and speak of your might, so that all men may know of your mighty acts and the glorious splendor of your kingdom. Your kingdom is an everlasting kingdom, and your dominion endures through all generations. The Lord is faithful to all his promises and loving towards all he has made. The Lord upholds all those who fall and lifts up all who are bowed down.*

# May

## EXODUS 4:28–31

*Then Moses told Aaron everything the Lord had sent him to say, and also about all the miraculous signs he had commanded him to perform. Moses and Aaron brought together all the elders of the Israelites, and Aaron told them everything the Lord had said to Moses. He also performed the signs before the people, and they believed. And when they heard that the Lord was concerned about them and had seen their misery, they bowed down and worshiped.*

Dear Lord,

Just as the people Moses and Aaron spoke to believed, I believe. Thank you for the Bible where You tell me You are concerned for me, You understand the miseries I suffer. I am humbled that the Creator of the Universe knows who I am, and cares for me. May I say and do everything You send me to say; may the pattern of my behavior be in line with Your Word. I worship You for Your merciful presence and provision.

# May

## 5

Dear Lord,

I believe without a doubt You are the God of gods, the Lord of lords—You are the one true God. You care about every soul, whether he or she believes in You. From that perspective, thank you You do not show partiality, but bless all. I especially thank you for loving the alien. For many reasons I often feel like an alien in this world. Help me discern others who feel the same way I do, and may I show them that Your love sustains my spirit when I feel I do not belong. Because regardless of all else, I belong to You.

### DEUTERONOMY 10:17–19A

*For the Lord your God is God of gods and Lord of lords, the great God, mighty and awesome, who shows no partiality and accepts no bribes. He defends the cause of the fatherless and the widow, and loves the alien, giving him food and clothing. And you are to love those who are aliens ...*

# May

# 6

## I SAMUEL 12:20–25

*"Do not be afraid," Samuel replied. "You have done all this evil; yet do not turn away from the Lord, but serve the Lord with all your heart. Do not turn away after useless idols. They can do you no good, nor can they rescue you, because they are useless. For the sake of his great name the Lord will not reject his people, because the Lord was pleased to make you his own. As for me, far be it from me that I should sin against the Lord by failing to pray for you. And I will teach you the way that is good and right. But be sure to fear the Lord and serve him faithfully with all your heart; consider what great things he has done for you. Yet if you persist in doing evil, both you and your king will be swept away."*

Dear Lord,

Idols are more than just fabricated gods; anything we hold of higher worth than You is an idol. Money, power, beauty, possessions, loved ones can become idolized and cause us to sin against You. Yet even when we are lost seeking fulfillment in other things, You call us back because You are pleased with Your creation. Though I may fail You, I need not fear, for at any time I may call upon You to rescue me from the idolatries in my life. May I keep You on the throne of my heart, love my family dearly, and place all else in the order of Your plans.

# May

# 7

Dear Lord,

Thank you for the reminder that only You know the hearts of men—no matter what my actions may say for a moment, You know the afflictions that influence me to act against the beliefs in my heart. I pray sincerely for Your forgiveness; I will listen, wait, and hear from heaven the instructions for continuing along Your path.

## I KINGS 8:38–40

*"… and when a prayer or plea is made by any of your people Israel—each one aware of the afflictions of his own heart, and spreading out his hands toward this temple—then hear from heaven, your dwelling place. Forgive and act; deal with each man according to all he does, since you know his heart (for you alone know the hearts of all men), so that they will fear you all the time they live in the land you gave our fathers."*

# May

# 8

## I KINGS 8:56–58, 61

*Praise be to the Lord, who has given rest to his people Israel just as he promised. Not one word has failed of all the good promises he gave through his servant Moses. May the Lord our God be with us as he was with our fathers; may he never leave us nor forsake us. May he turn our hearts to him, to walk in all his ways and to keep the commands, decrees and regulations he gave our fathers ... But your hearts must be fully committed to the Lord our God, to live by his decrees and obey his commands, as at this time.*

Dear Lord,

In times I am discouraged, dismayed and depressed, keep my heart turned towards You. May my heart remain fully committed to You, believing in all Your good promises. Walking in Your ways may not always seem possible, but to proceed alone without You is unimaginable.

# May

## 9

### 1 KINGS 19:11–12

Dear Lord,

The world, my responsibilities, my thoughts, my hopes, my fears can all be so loud and earth shattering, so fierce and overwhelming to my weary soul. Thank you for reminding me You are ever near me. Your gentle whisper quiets my soul, tunes out the earthly ruckus so we may fellowship together. You renew my strength; then I will hear from You the way I should go.

*The Lord said, "Go out and stand on the mountain in the presence of the Lord, for the Lord is about to pass by." Then a great and powerful wind tore the mountain apart and shattered the rocks before the Lord, but the Lord was not in the wind. After the wind there was an earthquake, but the Lord was not in the earthquake. After the earthquake came a fire, but the Lord was not in the fire. And after the fire came a gentle whisper.*

# May

# 10

## I CHRONICLES 28:9–10

*"And you, my son Solomon, acknowledge the God of your father, and serve him with wholehearted devotion and with a willing mind, for the Lord searches every heart and understands every motive behind the thoughts. If you seek him, he will be found by you; but if you forsake him, he will reject you forever. Consider now, for the Lord has chosen you to build a temple as a sanctuary. Be strong and do the work."*

Dear Lord,

I do my best to serve You wholeheartedly; search my heart and know that I seek Your will for my life. Enable me to be strong and do the work. Keep my motives pure and sincere, and my thoughts turned toward You. Thank you for choosing me as one of Your children.

# May

## 11

Dear Lord,

I pray You will keep my heart loyal to You. Do not let the pleasures nor the pains of this world lead me astray. Test my heart and help me maintain integrity and honest intent. My deepest desire is to remain willingly and joyfully devoted to You.

### I CHRONICLES 29:17–18

*I know, my God, that you test the heart and are pleased with integrity. All these things have I given willingly and with honest intent. And now I have seen with joy how willingly your people who are here have given to you. O Lord, God of our fathers Abraham, Isaac and Israel, keep this desire in the hearts of your people forever, and keep their hearts loyal to you.*

# May

# 12

## PROVERBS
3:19–22

*By wisdom the Lord laid the earth's foundation, by understanding he set the heavens in place; by his knowledge the deeps were divided, and the clouds let drop the dew. My son, preserve sound judgment and discernment, do not let them out of your sight; they will be life for you, an ornament to grace your neck.*

Dear Lord,

I believe you created the heavens and the earth—that Your unfathomable, infinite wisdom laid forth the foundation on which all life exists. How else could gravity hold all things to the earth, the earth be round and rugged from the highest mountain to the deepest sea. All Your Creation is intricately made, nourished with food from the earth and water from the sky. I seek teachable moments where You impress Your wisdom and knowledge upon my spirit, maturing within me sound judgment and spiritually led discernment. It is my desire to always stay within Your sight, for Your grace has brought me life from here to the hereafter.

## May

# 13

### PROVERBS
16:2–4,9

*All a man's ways seem innocent to him, but motives are weighed by the Lord. Commit to the Lord whatever you do, and your plans will succeed. The Lord works out everything for his own ends—even the wicked for a day of disaster ... In his heart a man plans his course, but the Lord determines his steps.*

Dear Lord,

I do my best to plan my life with Your guidance; yet some things can go horribly awry. Weigh my motives, know it is my heart's desire to be committed to You; be merciful to me. Review my plans, re-plot my course, direct me to move past debilitating disappointments and on to new hopes You have for my future. Order my steps towards the success You have planned for me, steering me away from spiritual disasters.

# May

# 14

## ECCLESIASTES
### 3:1–8

*There is a time for everything, and a season for every activity under heaven: a time to be born and a time to die, a time to plant and a time to uproot, a time to kill and a time to heal, a time to tear down and a time to build, a time to weep and a time to laugh, a time to mourn and a time to dance, a time to scatter stones and a time to gather them, a time to embrace and a time to refrain, a time to search and a time to give up, a time to keep and a time to throw away, a time to tear and a time to mend, a time to be silent and a time to speak, a time to love and a time to hate, a time for war and a time for peace.*

Dear Lord,

Thank you there is a time for everything, though it may not seem that way to our limited understanding. Time is in Your hands, from beginning to end. Help me be on Your time table; to know by the Holy Spirit's prompting when times are in conflict I am still in the shelter of Your wings, and You will guide me. When times are at their best, may I never forget to give You thanks and praise. May I spend time in frequent, sincere prayer seeking knowledge from You about the seasons in my life.

# May

# 15

## ECCLESIASTES
7:13–14

Dear Lord,

Explain this passage to me—if You make times both good and bad, why must there be bad at all? Why can't You make it all good? Why must we consider and suffer through bad times, maybe never discovering the purpose of past, present or future wounds? Nevertheless, let me survive the refining fire of trying times, knowing my eternal future is with You.

*Consider what God has done: Who can straighten what he has made crooked? When times are good, be happy; but when times are bad, consider: God has made one as well as the other. Therefore, a man cannot discover anything about his future.*

# May

# 16

**Song of Solomon
8:6–7**

*Place me like a seal over your heart, like a seal on your arm; for love is as strong as death, its jealousy unyielding as the grave. It burns like blazing fire, like a mighty flame. Many waters cannot quench love; rivers cannot wash it away. If one were to give all the wealth of his house for love, it would be utterly scorned.*

Dear Lord,

Love is powerful, tenacious, benevolent, humble, selfless, and priceless. It manifests itself through romance, passion, compassion, devotion, affection and respect. The purest form, however, is the unconditional love, agape love, mankind receives through Your Son Jesus Christ. Seal within my heart enduring love for You, may it never be washed away by daily cares and longsuffering worries. Rather than worldly riches, I pray You provide me with the immeasurable wealth of Your Loving Truth, and that its light burns brightly in my spirit for all to see. And though the grave may claim my body, I know my soul will live forever in Your Loving Presence.

# May

# 17

ISAIAH
1:18–20

Dear Lord,

Help me fine tune my reasoning skills by remembering to collaborate with You without fail. I will then be sure my choices reflect my willing, obedient spirit unto You. However, the times I fail to heed Your counsel and I sin, I humbly pray forgiveness. And the times my lone reasoning leaves me panicked and anxious, speak calm into my spirit. Remind me to come reason with You about my trials—then I shall overcome.

*"Come now, let us reason together," says the Lord. "Though your sins are like scarlet, they shall be as white as snow; though they are red as crimson, they shall be like wool. If you are willing and obedient, you will eat the best from the land; but if you resist and rebel, you will be devoured by the sword." For the mouth of the Lord has spoken.*

# May

# 18

ISAIAH 33:5–6,22

*The Lord is exalted, for he dwells on high; he will fill Zion with justice and righteousness. He will be the sure foundation for your times, a rich store of salvation and wisdom and knowledge; the fear of the Lord is the key to this treasure … For the Lord is our judge, the Lord is our lawgiver, the Lord is our King; it is he who will save us.*

Dear Lord,

Thank you for being my sure foundation, my rich storehouse of salvation, wisdom and knowledge. I understand You are the key to these treasures—there is no salvation without you Lord Jesus; no other foundation will stand; knowledge will amount to nothing without Your wisdom to guide its use. I fear judgment unless I have Your sacrificial covering to atone for my sins. I have learned Your laws are to protect my heart, soul and mind—help me to obey your statutes because I love you. Thank you for loving me first, and for being my Savior and King.

# May

# 19

Dear Lord,

We are so infinitesimally small compared to Your eternal Greatness. You do not need man nor creature to do anything for You—everything is already made and exists by Your Great Hand. Thank you for giving man knowledge of You, of how to use Your resources of land, water, air, plants and all kinds of creatures. Forgive us, I pray, when we are thoughtless with Your Creation. Rather teach us the right way to use Your provisions, giving You the praise and honor for Your innumerable blessings.

## ISAIAH 40:12–14, 17–18

*Who has measured the waters in the hollow of his hand, or with the breadth of his hand marked off the heavens? Who has held the dust of the earth in a basket, or weighed the mountains on the scales and the hills in a balance? Who has understood the mind of the Lord, or instructed him as his counselor? Whom did the Lord consult to enlighten him, and who taught him the right way? Who was it that taught him knowledge or showed him the path of understanding? ... Before him all nations are as nothing; they are regarded by him as worthless and less than nothing. To whom, then, will you compare God? What image will you compare him to?*

# May

# 20

### ISAIAH 49:14–16

*But Zion said, "The Lord has forsaken me, the Lord has forgotten me." Can a mother forget the baby at her breast and have no compassion on the child she has borne? Though she may forget, I will not forget you! See, I have engraved you on the palms of my hands; your walls are ever before me.*

Dear Lord,

Forgive me, but there are times I think You have forgotten me—that I am too inconsequential for Your compassion. Help me know that we are all God's children—individually. Though there are billions of us—there is each one of us. Just as we cannot comprehend how You created the world from nothing, we cannot comprehend how it is possible for You to love each and every soul individually; nevertheless, You do. Thank you!

# May
# 21

## ISAIAH 66:1–2

Dear Lord,

I am more than humbled when I reflect upon Heaven being Your throne and Earth is Your footstool; it is inconceivable there is anything of significance I can offer You. When I consider how overwhelmingly awe-inspiring, how limitless Your domain, our entire universe must be so small to You. How do I warrant Your attention? But then Your Spirit tells me—just as a speck of gold amongst mountains of dirt and rocks is valued, You value humbleness before You. You value that I tremble before Your awesome presence; I bow before you with a grateful heart. You are my resting place.

*This is what the Lord says: "Heaven is my throne, and the earth is my footstool. Where is the house you will build for me? Where will my resting place be? Has not my hand made all these things, and so they came into being?" declares the Lord. "This is the one I esteem: he who is humble and contrite in spirit, and trembles at my word."*

# May

# 22

## JEREMIAH
23:23–24,24:7–8

*"Am I only a God nearby,"
declares the Lord, "and not
a God far away? Can anyone
hide in secret places so that
I cannot see him?" declares
the Lord. "Do not I fill
heaven and earth?" declares
the Lord ... I will give them
a heart to know me, that I
am the Lord. They will be
my people, and I will be their
God, for they will return to
me with all their heart."*

Dear Lord,

I pray You give me a heart to
know You. May I sense Your
presence when You are near,
and know You are still here
when I feel you are far away.
When I am in the secret place,
hidden alone within my soul
where my highest hopes and
deepest despairs dwell, may I
know You dwell there too. You
care about what You alone see
hidden there—the genuine,
vulnerable me.

# May

# 23

### MATTHEW
### 6:33–34

Dear Lord,

I honestly seek Your will for my life, yet I struggle to provide just the basics for my children. So how can I not worry about tomorrow? Help me calm myself and recognize that we are okay for today; we have shelter, food, clothing today. Thank you for today's provision, and your assurance I can trust You for tomorrow's provision as well.

*But seek first his kingdom and his righteousness, and all these things will be given to you as well. Therefore do not worry about tomorrow, for tomorrow will worry about itself. Each day has enough trouble of its own.*

# May

# 24

## MATTHEW 16:13–17

*When Jesus came to the region of Caesarea Philippi, he asked his disciples, "Who do people say the Son of Man is?" They replied, "Some say John the Baptist; others say Elijah; and still others, Jeremiah or one of the prophets." "But what about you?" he asked. "Who do you say that I am?" Simon Peter answered, "You are the Christ, the Son of the living God." Jesus replied, "Blessed are you, Simon son of Jonah, for this was not revealed to you by man, but by my Father in heaven."*

Dear Lord,

Thank you for making us individuals; we live but one life in which to recognize Christ as the Son of God. You did not come here as a manifestation of the prophets who came before. They were compelled by the Heavenly Father to prepare the way for the Great and Final Prophet; the prophecy was fulfilled—Jesus is The Answer. We must each answer Jesus' question "Who do you say that I am?" I say that You are the great 'I am:' 'I am' your Salvation; 'I am' your Healer; 'I am' your Provider; 'I am' your Comforter; 'I am' your Peace; 'I am' the Way, the Truth and the Light—no one comes to the Father except through the Son.

# May

# 25

Dear Lord,

Thank you so much for Your sacrifice for my sins. It is beyond comprehension that You suffered at the hands of religious leaders—those who should have known better. Oh to have lived in Your time and physically been in Your presence! They should have bowed down before You, ready to receive the out-pouring of Your Holy Spirit. The elders, priests, teachers of the Law were concerned about the things of man—which was for these men of stature to remain in power. May I be concerned with the things of God, which is yielding to the Power of the Holy Spirit.

## MATTHEW 16:21–23

*From that time on Jesus began to explain to his disciples that he must go to Jerusalem and suffer many things at the hands of the elders, chief priests and teachers of the law, and that he must be killed and on the third day be raised to life. Peter took him aside and began to rebuke him. "Never Lord!" he said. "This shall never happen to you!" Jesus turned and said to Peter, "Get behind me, Satan! You are a stumbling block to me; you do not have in mind the things of God, but the things of men."*

# May

# 26

## MATTHEW 22:36–40

*"Teacher, which is the greatest commandment in the Law." Jesus replied: "Love the Lord your God with all your heart and with all your soul and with all your mind. This is the first and greatest commandment. And the second is like it: 'Love your neighbor as yourself.' All the Law and the Prophets hang on these two commandments."*

Dear Lord,

These commandments initially seem so simple—until 'self' gets in the way. Other needs and desires of my heart try to usurp Your rightful throne there; worldly teachings try to tell me I do not even have a soul from which to pray; my mind has information overload and I allow the taxing daily survival demands to stop me from studying Your Word. Most important, however, I do remember this Greatest Command to love You above all else, and I try each day to be governed by it. And next in importance is to love both others … and myself. It's a struggle to love myself. I know not to be a selfish person, but my downfall is putting others before even my basic needs, and essentially risk, once again, being a human doormat. Your Spirit reminds me that both I and others are equally valued children of God, therefore You want me to acknowledge I have worth the same as the rest of Your Creation. Thank you, Lord, for this blessing.

Dear Lord,

I often feel alone; alone even when others are physically about. You often withdrew to lonely places to pray. Even when You were with Your disciples in Gethsemane, it was a lonely place for You—they could not keep watch because of exhaustion. You were alone with God in lonely Gethsemane, preparing for Your final darkest hours. Help me use my many solitary times to feel Your Holy Spirit, realizing the value of being alone in Your Presence. May I constantly watch and pray that in my aloneness I do not give in to temptation and find comfort in sinful worldly things, rather I will enter into my heart's prayer room, meeting again with the One who always keeps watch over my soul.

# May

# 27

## MATTHEW 26:36–41

*Then Jesus went with his disciples to a place called Gethsemane, and he said to them, "Sit here while I go over there and pray." He took Peter and the two sons of Zebedee along with him, and he began to be sorrowful and troubled. Then he said to them, "My soul is overwhelmed with sorrow to the point of death. Stay here and keep watch with me." Going a little farther, he fell with his face to the ground and prayed, "My Father, if it is possible, may this cup be taken from me. Yet not as I will, but as you will." Then he returned to his disciples and found them sleeping. "Could you men not keep watch with me for one hour?" he asked Peter. "Watch and pray so that you will not fall into temptation. The spirit is willing, but the body is weak."*

# May

# 28

## LUKE 1:46–55

*And Mary said: "My soul glorifies the Lord and my spirit rejoices in God my Savior, for he has been mindful of the humble state of his servant. From now on all generations will call me blessed, for the Mighty One has done great things for me—holy is his name. His mercy extends to those who fear him, from generation to generation. He has performed mighty deeds with his arm; he has scattered those who are proud in their inmost thoughts. He has brought down the rulers from their thrones but has lifted up the humble. He has filled the hungry with good things but has sent the rich away empty. He has helped his servant Israel, remembering to be merciful to Abraham and his descendants forever, even as he said to our fathers."*

Dear Lord,

Mindful. Who am I that the God of all Creation is mindful of me? It amazes me I am on Your mind as I go about my day. I am deeply humbled Your presence fills my life; I am so thankful for Your mercy, which extends from generation to generation. It lifts me up to serve You. You have performed mighty deeds in my life, providing good things for which I am truly grateful. May I live my life to bring honor to Your Holy Name.

# May

# 29

## LUKE 22:15–20

Dear Lord,

Thank you for Your broken body and Your shed blood that was for my sin. Your human body was beaten, Your life's blood poured out at the Cross because of me. As in the day of Moses, when during the last Egyptian plague a lamb's blood marked the Israelites' doorways for God's wrath to pass over them, Your blood covers and cleanses my soul from unrighteousness. Because I believe in Your crucifixion and Your resurrection, God's wrath will pass over me in the last day. No longer are lambs sacrificed for transgressions; You are the Lamb slain for the sins of all Mankind. Like the disciples, I humbly partake of Communion with the emblems of the bread and the wine, as you instructed us to do in remembrance of Your ultimate sacrifice.

*And he said to them, "I have eagerly desired to eat this Passover with you before I suffer. For I tell you, I will not eat it again until it finds fulfillment in the kingdom of God." After taking the cup, he gave thanks and said, "Take this and divide it among you. For I tell you I will not drink again of the fruit of the vine until the kingdom of God comes." And he took bread, gave thanks and broke it, and gave it to them, saying, "This is my body given for you; do this in remembrance of me." In the same way, after the supper he took the cup, saying, "This cup is the new covenant in my blood, which is poured out for you."*

# May

# 30

## LUKE 22:31–34, 59–62

*"Simon, Simon, Satan has asked to sift you as wheat. But I have prayed for you, Simon, that your faith may not fail. And when you have turned back, strengthen your brothers." But he replied, "Lord, I am ready to go with you to prison and to death." Jesus answered, "I tell you, Peter, before the rooster crows today, you will deny three times that you know me." ... [soldiers seize Jesus] ... About an hour later another asserted, "Certainly this fellow was with him, for he is a Galilean." Peter replied, "Man, I don't know what you're talking about!" Just as he was speaking, the rooster crowed. The Lord turned and looked straight at Peter. Then Peter remembered the word the Lord had spoken to him: "Before the rooster crows today, you will disown me three times." And he went outside and wept bitterly.*

Dear Lord,

Deep in my heart there is always the determination to follow Your straight path unto death. Then something happens that makes me stumble, so my actions do not mirror the determination in my heart. Pray for me, as You did for Simon. After I have been sifted through trials, tribulations, or even triumphs, let my faith fail not, but after I have repented, wept bitterly, then I will rejoice in Your forgiveness that fails not. And I pray I will find that my faith has been strengthened by the experiences, as is Your purpose.

# May

# 31

## JOHN 3:16–21

Dear Lord,

John 3:16, the most well-known and beloved Scripture of all time. You love us so much You sacrificed what is most precious, Your one and only Son. Once we believe in Him, we are no long spiritually condemned without God, rather we enter into Your Light for all Eternity. Your Truth teaches me Your commands are for my benefit and protection against the enemy. It is in our nature to be selfish, and we give in to sinful deeds. Shine Your light into my life to expose what I have done that does not glorify You, so I may ask forgiveness, and grant me Your wisdom to continue in the Light so it is plain to all that You are my God and Savior.

*"For God so loved the world that he gave his one and only Son, that whoever believes in him shall not perish but have eternal life. For God did not send his Son into the world to condemn the world, but to save the world through him. Whoever believes in him is not condemned, but whoever does not believe stands condemned already because he has not believed in the name of God's one and only Son. This is the verdict: Light has come into the world, but men loved darkness instead of light because their deeds were evil. Everyone who does evil hates the light, and will not come into the light for fear that his deeds will be exposed. But whoever lives by the truth comes into the light, so that it may be seen plainly that what he has done has been done through God."*

# June

## 1

### JOHN 18:33–37

*Pilate then went back inside the palace, summoned Jesus and asked him, "Are you the king of the Jews?" "Is that your own idea," Jesus asked, "or did others talk to you about me?" "Am I a Jew?" Pilate replied. "It was your people and your chief priests who handed you over to me. What is it you have done?" Jesus said, "My kingdom is not of this world. If it were, my servants would fight to prevent my arrest by the Jews. But now my kingdom is from another place." "You are a king, then!" said Pilate. Jesus answered, "You are right in saying I am a king. In fact, for this reason I was born, and for this I came into the world, to testify to the truth. Everyone on the side of truth listens to me."*

Dear Lord,

Pilate, a non-believer, found no fault in You, but Your own people would not testify to the Truth. The Jews had been waiting for the day God the Father would send the long-awaited Messiah, God the Son, to free them from the rule of other nations. They refused to recognize You: though seemingly only a simple carpenter's son, in truth, You are the Christ, the King from another place—the eternal spiritual realm. They wanted deliverance today; not understanding that the Kingdom of God is permanent deliverance, not just temporary deliverance from an earthly foe. In their pride and jealousy, the chief priests conspiring to have You killed, because keeping the power they held over the Jewish people was of utmost importance to them. As for me, I am on the side of Your Truth. You are the King of my heart and soul, and I humbly await the day You return for Your believers.

# June

# 2

Dear Lord,

Thank you for Your immeasurable gift of salvation through Jesus Christ, the One who bore the sins of the world, covering believers with His cleansing blood, leaving His righteousness in sin's place. I do not want to be disobedient to Your Word—yet I find myself trespassing despite my best intentions, despite my clear knowledge of sin vs. righteousness. I need Your grace—where my sin remains, I pray Your grace remains growing stronger within my spirit until the sin that binds me to unrighteousness is put to death. Then I may live free, unencumbered by this world, and at peace in Your Presence.

## ROMANS 5:19–6:2

*For just as through the disobedience of the one man the many were made sinners, so also through obedience of the one man the many will be made righteous. The law was added so that the trespass might increase. But where sin increased, grace increased all the more, so that, just as sin reigned in death, so also grace might reign through righteousness to bring eternal life through Jesus Christ our Lord. What shall we say then? Shall we go on sinning so that grace may increase? By no means! We died to sin; how can we live in it any longer?*

# June

# 3

## ROMANS 8:1–5

*Therefore, there is now no condemnation for those who are in Christ Jesus, because through Christ Jesus the law of the Spirit of life set me free from the law of sin and death. For what the law was powerless to do in that it was weakened by the sinful nature, God did by sending his own Son in the likeness of sinful man to be a sin offering. And so he condemned sin in sinful man, in order that the righteous requirements of the law might be fully met in us, who do not live according to the sinful nature but according to the Spirit. Those who live according to the sinful nature have their minds set on what that nature desires; but those who live in accordance with the Spirit have their minds set on what the Spirit desires.*

Dear Lord,

Thank you that through Your sacrifice I am set free, no longer condemned by my sinful nature. God's holiness requires sacrifice for sin; in Old Testament times there were so many laws of what to sacrifice for which sin. However, You sent your Son to be the final sacrificial Lamb for the sins of all mankind. Through Jesus' human death and spiritual resurrection, we are empowered by Your Spirit to live righteous lives. Though our sinful nature's desires derails us at times, living according to Your Holy Spirit brings us back to You, our contrite hearts the only sin offering required. I serve You not out of fear based on a list of do's and don'ts which condemn me, rather I serve You out of love and thanksgiving for Your mercy and grace. My mind is set upon living for You.

# June

## 4

**ROMANS**
8:16–18

Dear Lord,

There are many sufferings I do not understand—why are they necessary? Why can they not be prevented, avoided? We bring some upon ourselves, but other sufferings are senseless. And since we are Your children, why do You not shield us all the time? Then You remind me I cannot shield my children from everything because we live in this imperfect world and we have personal choice. Now I see why You do not shield us from everything—choice. Our choices have consequences for ourselves and others. While sometimes You protect, other times You use suffering to strengthen my faith and character. When I feel the suffering is beyond my ability, help me understand it is nothing compared to the glory to come with You in Eternity.

*The Spirit himself testifies with our spirit that we are God's children. Now if we are children, then we are heirs—heirs of God and co-heirs with Christ, if indeed we share in his sufferings in order that we may also share in his glory. I consider that our present sufferings are not worth comparing with the glory that will be revealed to us.*

# June

# 5

## II CORINTHIANS
2:14–16

*But thanks be to God, who always leads us in triumphal procession in Christ and through us spreads everywhere the fragrance of the knowledge of him. For we are to God the aroma of Christ among those who are being saved and those who are perishing. To the one we are the smell of death; to the other, the fragrance of life.*

Dear Lord,

I often get so deep into my own problems, I forget the most important aspect of my life—that I am part of Your spiritual army headed for the ultimately triumphant procession into Heaven. The way I handle problems should be such that it glorifies You so others will see You in me. Let my reactive and proactive behaviors be spiritual aroma therapy for those around me.

# June

# 6

Dear Lord,

Thank you for giving me a spirit to commune with you, a deposit on my heavenly body. This earthly body gets bone tired, burdened with aches, ailments, and injuries that I must bear up under while I am in the flesh. Yet because of the believer's ability to commune spirit to Spirit, I know and understand from Your Word that You made me for Your eternal companionship and to forever worship You. Someday, when I leave this fleshly body behind, I will be at home in my eternal body, pain free and full of Your energy.

## II CORINTHIANS 5:1,4–6

*Now we know that if the earthly tent we live in is destroyed, we have a building from God, an eternal house in heaven, not built by human hands ... For while we are in this tent, we groan and are burdened, because we do not wish to be unclothed but to be clothed with our heavenly dwelling, so that what is mortal may be swallowed up by life. Now it is God who has made us for this purpose and has given us the Spirit as a deposit, guaranteeing what is to come. Therefore we are always confident and know that as long as we are at home in the body we are away from the Lord.*

# June

# 7

## II CORINTHIANS 7:9–11

*-yet now I am happy, not because you were made sorry, but because your sorrow led you to repentance. For you became sorrowful as God intended and so were not harmed in any way by us. Godly sorrow brings repentance that leads to salvation and leaves no regret, but worldly sorrow brings death. See what this godly sorrow has produced in you: what earnestness, what eagerness to clear yourselves, what indignation, what alarm, what longing, what concern, what readiness to see justice done.*

Dear Lord,

Thank you for sorrow that brings me to repentance. Help me know the difference between godly and worldly sorrow. Please forgive my sins of commission and omission, and keep me from carrying around unnecessary guilt for things out of my control. May I earnestly seek You, eagerly follow Your lead; I long to remain in close fellowship with You, and maintain readiness for Your Purpose.

# June

## 8

Dear Lord,

Help me to stand for you, whether in calm or in chaos. As I once heard in a sermon, my armor may be dented and bent from many a blow, but I will stand my ground, continually renewing and reinforcing my armor through time spent with You. Heal my wounds, I pray, even those I could have prevented if I had not let my guard down. Keep my motives pure and my fervor for You ever true.

### EPHESIANS 6:13–17

*Therefore put on the full armor of God, so that when the day of evil comes, you may be able to stand your ground, and after you have done everything, to stand. Stand firm then, with the belt of truth buckled around your waist, with the breastplate of righteousness in place, and with your feet fitted with the readiness that comes from the gospel of peace. In addition to all this, take up the shield of faith, with which you can extinguish all the flaming arrows of the evil one. Take the helmet of salvation and the sword of the Spirit, which is the Word of God.*

# June

# 9

### PHILIPPIANS 3:8–11

*What is more, I consider everything a loss compared to the surpassing greatness of knowing Christ Jesus my Lord, for whose sake I have lost all things. I consider them rubbish, that I may gain Christ and be found in him, not having a righteousness of my own that comes from the law, but that which is through faith in Christ—the righteousness that comes from God and is by faith. I want to know Christ and the power of his resurrection and the fellowship of sharing his sufferings, becoming like him in his death, and so, somehow, to attain to the resurrection from the dead.*

Dear Lord,

Help me understand there is nothing more valuable than knowing You, Christ Jesus, as my Lord and Savior. For if I do not—all is lost. No matter how good, or moral, or ethical, or virtuous I think I am, the only real righteousness comes from God, from faith in Christ's resurrection after dying to cover my sins. I want to truly know Your suffering, Your power, Your heart for mankind so I am a willing servant who listens to Your voice, following Your leading unto the day I see Your face.

# June

# 10

### PHILIPPIANS
### 3:18–21

Dear Lord,

It weighs on my spirit that there are non-believers, or worse, those who are enemies of Christ. It grieves my spirit their destination is destruction without accepting Christ; I know there is an after-life—in heaven or hell. Those who have not chosen Christ as Savior will go to eternity without Him—in hell; however, a believer's citizenship is in heaven. When the time comes, Christ will return for His own. Just as He had a glorious new body upon Resurrection, He will transform our lowly earthly bodies, whether we have fallen asleep in Him or are alive and caught up to meet Him in the air. That is a glorious day I do not want to miss! Praise the Lord!

*For, as I have often told you before and now say again even with tears, many live as enemies of the cross of Christ. Their destiny is destruction, their god is their stomach, and their glory is in their shame. Their mind is on earthly things. But our citizenship is in heaven. And we eagerly await a Savior from there, the Lord Jesus Christ, who, by the power that enables him to bring everything under his control, will transform our lowly bodies so that they will be like his glorious body.*

# June

# 11

## PHILIPPIANS 4:11–13

*I am not saying this because I am in need, for I have learned to be content whatever the circumstances. I know what it is to be in need, and I know what it is to have plenty. I have learned the secret of being content in any and every situation, whether well fed or hungry, whether living in plenty or in want. I can do all this through him who gives me strength.*

Dear Lord,

I know what it is to be in need and to have plenty; I am sorry I struggle with being content when I have unmet needs—or are they unmet wants? Thank you for reminding me the secret to being content in both situations is to trust in Your strength, not my own. It is not that I should necessarily be content in being without necessities, rather to be content knowing that You are my Provider, You will see me through all circumstances.

# June

# 12

### PHILIPPIANS
4:19–20

*And my God will meet all your needs according to his glorious riches in Christ Jesus. To our God and Father be glory forever and ever. Amen.*

Dear Lord,

I know you met my eternal soul's need for a Savior in Jesus Christ—and that is the most important need of all. I'm sorry, I do not feel my emotional needs are met; I feel adrift and alone. Let me feel Your presence richly in this moment, in every moment let me know I am not alone. Lord, help me embrace that You will meet all my needs I have while in this earthly realm. May the way I live with unmet needs or wants show others my hope and trust is in my God. You are more than able to provide for my soul, my heart, my mind and my body.

# June

## 13

### COLOSSIANS
1:15–17

*He is the image of the invisible God, the firstborn over all creation. For by him all things were created: things in heaven and on earth, visible and invisible, whether thrones or powers or rulers or authorities; all things were created by him and for him. He is before all things, and in him all things hold together.*

Dear Lord,

I believe Jesus Christ, Your Son, is the image of the invisible God. He is the firstborn of creation—He was with You as You breathed the Holy Spirit into nothingness to create all life. All things in heaven and earth, what we see with our eyes, what we can only feel with other senses, like the mighty wind, all of it was created by Your command, for Your pleasure, including every one of us. When the earthly powers that be make the world seem so out of control, whether it be another country's wicked rulers or criminals local authorities cannot contain, help me remember You were before all things, You created all things, and **in You all things will hold together**.

# June

# 14

Dear Lord,

Thank you for making peace with Your creation through Your Son. I do not know how to express how sorry I am Jesus suffered for my sins; help me serve You faithfully, in love and appreciation for His shed blood. He pleased You, His Heavenly Father, by being fully God and fully man, come to earth so all men may know The Way to be reconciled to the one True God. Jesus Christ is the head of the Christian church. I believe Your Word when it says He is the first-born of the dead: He died on the cross, but rose from the dead three days later in victory over death and the grave, to return to heaven, yet remain living in the hearts of believers through the Holy Spirit.

## COLOSSIANS
1:18–20

*And he is the head of the body, the church; he is the beginning and the firstborn from among the dead, so that in everything he might have the supremacy. For God was pleased to have all his fullness dwell in him, and through him to recon-cile to himself all things, whether things on earth or things in heaven, by making peace through his blood, shed on the cross.*

# June

# 15

## COLOSSIANS 2:6–9

*So then, just as you received Christ Jesus as Lord, continue to live in him, rooted and built up in him, strengthened in the faith as you were taught, and overflowing with thankfulness. See to it that no one takes you captive through hollow and deceptive philosophy, which depends on human tradition and the basic principles of this world rather than on Christ. For in Christ all the fullness of the Deity lives in bodily form, and you have been given fullness in Christ, who is the head over every power and authority.*

Dear Lord,

Thank you for impressing on my spirit to accept Christ as my Savior. My heart and soul overflow with thankfulness many times over for salvation and Your constant presence in my life. Remind me to continually deepen my roots in You, building my faith through Your Word, worship, church attendance and other Bible-based devotionals. Keep me from being led astray by worldly philosophies which use bits and pieces of Your Word, only those which suits its purpose. Or use none of the Bible, rather only feel good language ignoring eternal consequences. May I always hold on to the truth that it is the Lord God alone who has all power and authority in my life; more so He is over all the powers and authorities in this world.

Dear Lord,

Because of Jesus Christ, I need only make the good confession before You, God, that You are King of Kings and Lord of Lords. I do not have to go before Pontius Pilate, a Priest, nor a Pastor to make the confession of faith. I need only believe on the Lord Jesus Christ and I am saved; I confess my sins before You as You alone may cleanse my soul from unrighteousness. And because I live by faith, others witness Your presence in my life. I began my Christian walk so many years ago as a small child in Sunday School, repeating the sinner's prayer every time it was offered to be completely sure You and I both knew I believed, though I know You entered into my heart upon the very first invitation. Daily I pursue living a godly life of faith, endurance and gentleness unto that day when our Lord Jesus Christ returns for His believers, and will take us to Eternity with Him.

# June

# 16

## I TIMOTHY 6:11–14

*But you, man of God, flee from all this, and pursue righteousness, godliness, faith, love, endurance and gentleness. Fight the good fight of the faith. Take hold of the eternal life to which you were called when you made your good confession in the presence of many witnesses. In the sight of God, who gives life to everything, and of Christ Jesus, who while testifying before Pontius Pilate made the good confession, I charge you to keep this command without spot or blame until the appearing of our Lord Jesus Christ.*

# June

# 17

## II TIMOTHY 3:14–17

*But as for you, continue in what you have learned and have become convinced of, because you know those from whom you learned it, and how from infancy you have known the holy Scriptures, which are able to make you wise for salvation through faith in Christ Jesus. All Scripture is God-breathed and is useful for teaching, rebuking, correcting and training in righteousness, so that the man of God may be thoroughly equipped for every good work.*

Dear Lord,

Thank you for convincing me that the Holy Bible is God-breathed, that its Scriptures hold the true wisdom of Your Word and Your Way—salvation through Jesus Christ. There are those who say there are many paths to God; how do I know which is right, how do I know this is the only way? Because I know from whom I have learned it—the Holy Word of God, which tells me of the Trinity: God the Father, God the Son, and God the Holy Spirit. Once God the Holy Spirit reveals the Truth through Scripture, we know faith in God the Son is the Only Way to salvation. Some other paths may start with the Old Testament, but they miss Christ the Messiah in the New Testament, the Only Way to God the Father. Many others start with false gods, including elevating self as a god, and those paths truly lead nowhere except eternal darkness. It is only the Holy Bible that will train, rebuke, correct, and thoroughly equip us to do the Lord's work, if only we accept the Truth living on each page.

Dear Lord,

May I never forget that You saved me, not because of any worthy thing I have ever done, but because of Your great mercy. When I accepted Christ, my soul was reborn, and is renewed daily by the work of the Holy Spirit. As is your Will, I will be obedient to those in authority, and ask You to provide wisdom and discernment when difficulties arise between the dictates of authority and the Sovereign law of my Lord. When I am wronged by others, please help me to respond carefully, as it may be a time You have called me to be merciful rather than expect justice, just as You are merciful to me when I transgress. May I respond to animosity and hate with patience, calm and kindness, showing humility as is Your desire. My desire, whatever my circumstances, is for the love of the Lord be evident in the way I live my life.

# June

## 18

### TITUS 3:1–5A

*Remind the people to be subject to rulers and authorities, to be obedient, to be ready to do whatever is good, to slander no one, to be peaceable and considerate, and to show true humility toward all men. At one time we too were foolish, disobedient, deceived and enslaved by all kinds of passions and pleasures. We lived in malice and envy, being hated and hating one another. But when the kindness and love of God our Savior appeared, he saved us, not because of righteous things we had done, but because of his mercy.*

# June

# 19

## HEBREWS 9:25–28

*Nor did he enter heaven to offer himself again and again, the way the high priest enters the Most Holy Place every year with blood that is not his own. Then Christ would have had to suffer many times since the creation of the world. But now he has appeared once for all at the end of the ages to do away with sin by the sacrifice of himself. Just as man is destined to die once, and after that to face judgment, so Christ was sacrificed once to take away the sins of many people; and he will appear a second time, not to bear sin, but to bring salvation to those who are waiting for him.*

Dear Lord,

I am so sorry You suffered so horribly for my sins; the sins of all humanity. Words cannot express how humbled and in awe I am that the Creator of Heaven and Earth would become man, to die our destiny in order to save us from ourselves, so that when we face the judgment to come, Christ is already there to cover the believers with His robe of righteousness and mercy. Now there is no temple with a Most Holy Place—when we are in sincere worship in Your presence anywhere, in Your presence is the Most Holy Place.

# June

# 20

Dear Lord,

Thank you that I am able to start over with a clean slate because of Your sacrifice. Because of You, I am being made holy as I sincerely seek to follow and serve You. 'Being made,' not there yet, but You are working on me. You are filling my heart and mind with Your laws to protect me, and I understand they are for my own good. The longer I live, the more obvious these truths become. And when I am forgiven, You remember my sin and lawlessness no more—no more sacrifice is needed. I do not need to stay unforgiving towards myself either; I can follow Your lead to be compassionate with myself.

## HEBREWS 10:14–18

*… because by one sacrifice he has made perfect forever those who are being made holy. The Holy Spirit also testifies to us about this. First he says: "This is the covenant I will make with them after that time, says the Lord. I will put my laws in their hearts, and I will write them on their minds." Then he adds: "Their sins and lawless acts I will remember no more." And where these have been forgiven, there is no longer any sacrifice for sin.*

# June

# 21

## JAMES 2:10–12

*For whoever keeps the whole law and yet stumbles at just one point is guilty of breaking all of it. For he who said, "Do not commit adultery," also said, "Do not murder." If you do not commit adultery but do commit murder, you have become a law breaker. Speak and act as those who are going to be judged by the law that gives freedom, because judgment without mercy will be shown to anyone who has not been merciful. Mercy triumphs over judgment.*

Dear Lord,

Thank you for being Three in One, God the Father, God the Son, and God the Holy Spirit. Thank you God the Father who gave us the Law, and also gave us God the Son, Jesus Christ, who brought us Mercy. And Mercy, which, by faith in Jesus Christ, saves us from judgment. Thank you God the Son, Jesus Christ, that when You returned to Your throne, You sent us God the Holy Spirit to dwell within the believer's heart and soul, teaching us how to live in the freedom of grace and mercy. We keep the Law through love rather than through fear of judgment, which empowers us to be gracious and merciful to others.

# June

## 22

Dear Lord,

Thank you for Your grace, I am humble before You. I resist the devil's countless suggestions of disobedience by drawing close to You, though I still stumble. It is only by Your grace and nothing in myself that will save my soul. I call out to Jesus, my Intercessor before the Father, my Counselor who dries my tears, my Peace amidst the storm, and the Lifter of my head, after I repent and You forgive. Yes, Lord, You lift me up in body, spirit and soul when I humbly bow before You.

### JAMES 4:6–10

*But he gives us more grace. That is why Scripture says: "God opposes the proud but gives grace to the humble." Submit yourselves, then, to God. Resist the devil, and he will flee from you. Come near to God and he will come near to you. Wash your hands, you sinners, and purify your hearts, you double-minded. Grieve, mourn and wail. Change your laughter to mourning and your joy to gloom. Humble yourselves before the Lord, and he will lift you up.*

# June

# 23

## 1 PETER 1:18–21

*For you know that it was not with perishable things such as silver or gold that you were redeemed from the empty way of life handed down to you from your forefathers, but with the precious blood of Christ, a lamb without blemish or defect. He was chosen before the creation of the world, but was revealed in these last times for your sake. Through him you believe in God, who raised him from the dead and glorified him, and so your faith and hope are in God.*

Dear Lord,

I will never fully understand the depth of Your character—the Holy God who gave His only begotten Son as the Sacrifice for His creation, Man. My life would be empty and void of meaning without Your presence and deep abiding love. There is no treasure on earth, no precious metal, no wonder of the world that can be compared to the precious atoning blood of Jesus Christ. Thank You for cleansing my soul, redeeming me to eternal life through faith and hope in You!

# June

# 24

Dear Lord,

You are my foundation, the Rock of my Salvation, the Holy Priest living in my heart. Your Word guides me through the maze of life, providing for my needs, my hopes, my dreams, my heartaches. Your love builds up my spirit, giving me strength to face all the challenges, and instilling humble thankfulness for all Your blessings. Though others reject You, refusing to believe in Your Deity, I <u>know</u> you are the precious cornerstone of all Life: today, yesterday, and forever more.

## 1 PETER 2:4–6

*As you come to him, the living Stone—rejected by men but chosen by God and precious to him—you also, like living stones, are being built into a spiritual house to be a holy priesthood, offering spiritual sacrifices acceptable to God through Jesus Christ. For in the Scripture it says: "See, I lay a stone in Zion, a chosen and precious cornerstone, and the one who trusts in him will never be put to shame."*

# June

# 25

## I PETER 2:22–25

*"He committed no sin, and no deceit was found in his mouth." When they hurled their insults at him, he did not retaliate; when he suffered, he made no threats. Instead, he entrusted himself to him who judges justly. He himself bore our sins in his body on a tree, so that we might die to sins and live for righteousness; by his wounds you have been healed. For you were like sheep going astray, but now you have returned to the Shepherd and Overseer of your souls.*

Dear Lord,

Thank you for Jesus, God the Son, who bore my sins and heals my soul. I pray to be a sheep who resists being lead astray; rather may I follow my Shepherd anywhere at any cost. Help me entrust my life's trials and triumphs to You. If others treat me unjustly—may I look to You, the One who defines Justice. When I suffer for others or my own actions, help me to look to You, who is molding in me a Christ-like character. Oversee my soul, lead me into the joy that comes only from walking with You and in Your righteousness.

# June

# 26

Dear Lord,

My troubles certainly humble me—making me feel inadequate, unimportant. Help me understand that being humble before You should not make me feel even more humiliation, rather it's the humility that means I have a deep and abiding respect for You—and You want to relieve me of my anxiety because You care for me.

## I PETER 5:5b–7

*All of you, clothe yourselves with humility toward one another, because, "God opposed the proud but gives grace to the humble." Humble yourselves, therefore, under God's mighty hand, that he may lift you up in due time. Cast all your anxiety on him because he cares for you.*

# June

# 27

### 1 JOHN 1:8–10, 2:1–2

*If we claim to be without sin, we deceive ourselves and the truth is not in us. If we confess our sins, he is faithful and just and will forgive us our sins and purify us from all unrighteousness. If we claim we have not sinned, we make him out to be a liar and his word has no place in our lives. My dear children, I write this to you so that you will not sin. But if anybody does sin, we have one who speaks to the Father in our defense—Jesus Christ, the Righteous One. He is the atoning sacrifice for our sins, and not only for ours but also for the sins of the whole world.*

Dear Lord,

Thank you for Your Spirit's prompting to keep me from sin, and Your atoning sacrifice to redeem my soul when I do. When I turn my head, perhaps deliberately not looking close enough to stop sinful behavior, may Your Spirit stop me from deceiving myself. Only You are without sin; I need to be honest with myself, confess my sin to receive Your purification, Your righteous covering. My prayer is to know Your Truth and for it to become nearer and dearer each day.

# June

# 28

Dear Lord,

Sin breeds disorder and lawlessness into my life. I want to obey Your commands, not because there are laws that should not be broken, rather because living in You brings order, peace, love into my life. You clothed Yourself in flesh to take away my sin, gave me new life when I was born into Your kingdom through accepting Jesus Christ as my Savior. Your Spirit living in me provides me discernment to make the right choices which keep me from sinning; I strive to live in the Light of Your Truth.

## I JOHN 3:4–9

*Everyone who sins breaks the law; in fact, sin is lawlessness. But you know that he appeared so that he might take away our sin. And in him there is no sin. No one who lives in him keeps on sinning. No one who continues to sin has either seen him or known him. Dear children, do not let anyone lead you astray. He who does what is right is righteous, just as he is righteous. He who does what is sinful is of the devil, because the devil has been sinning from the beginning. The reason the Son of God appeared was to destroy the devil's work. No one who is born of God will continue to sin, because God's seed remains in him; he cannot go on sinning, because he is born of God.*

# June

# 29

## I JOHN 4:7–10

*Dear friends, let us love one another, for love comes from God. Everyone who loves has been born of God and knows God. Whoever does not love does not know God, because God is love. This is how God showed his love among us: he sent his one and only Son into the world that we might live through him. This is love: not that we loved God, but that he loved us and sent his Son as an atoning sacrifice for our sins.*

Dear Lord,

Thank you for loving me so much You sent Your Son as an atonement for my sins. In honor of Your love and His sacrifice, and subsequent victory over death, my heart's desire is to follow You with my mind, body and spirit. May I follow Your examples of love shown to me throughout Your Word. Out of Your love, show me my sins so that out of love for You I may repent, continually living in the light of Your love.

# June

# 30

## 1 JOHN 4:11–16

Dear Lord,

I rely on You completely for all my needs, though my humanness may stray in directions I try not to go—worry, despair, anxiousness. Your Spirit lets me know without trials and tribulation I could not love others as You have commanded. Having felt the pain, my empathy can help get them through—especially since I give You the glory for my deliverance. I pray they will turn to You for salvation, love and life.

*Dear friends, since God so loved us, we also ought to love one another. No one has ever seen God; but if we love one another, God lives in us and his love is made complete in us. We know that we live in him and he in us, because he has given us his Spirit. And we have seen and testify that the Father has sent his Son to be the Savior of the world. If anyone acknowledges that Jesus is the Son of God, God lives in him and he in God. And so we know and rely on the love God has for us.*

194

# Believe in Blessings

# July

## 1

Dear Lord,

I praise You for Your counsel, for Your instruction that leads my life. There are times I am shaken by situations and circumstances; yet I set You before me. Please help me still see You near and not allow my vision to be clouded by fears, difficulties, failures. I place my confidence in You daily; hour by hour, moment by moment, second by second.

### PSALM 16: 7–8

*I will praise the Lord, who counsels me; even at night my heart instructs me. I have set the Lord always before me. Because he is at my right hand, I will not be shaken.*

# July

# 2

### PSALM 27:11–14

*Teach me your way, O Lord; lead me in a straight path because of my oppressors. Do not turn me over to the desire of my foes, for false witnesses rise up against me, breathing out violence. I am still confident of this: I will see the goodness of the Lord in the land of the living. Wait for the Lord; be strong and take heart and wait for the Lord.*

Dear Lord,

When I feel oppressed by those around me or circumstances I perceive to be beyond my control, continue to lead me on Your straight path. Help me maintain my confidence in Your goodness regardless of the situation. I know I need to wait and obey Your leading—help me have the strength and endurance to triumph over all the challenges when they rise up against me.

# July

## 3

### PSALM 33:13–22

Dear Lord,

Form my heart, mold it to Your likeness. Please consider everything I do, know that I want Your influence to show in all of my life. Thank you for telling me the battle does not always go to the obvious, the biggest army nor the strongest warrior do not always win. Rather it is who trusts in You who is delivered. You are my help as I struggle considering what I should do; and while I may not always make the best or right decisions, I am always hoping in You to lead me the way I should go from here. Your presence in my life is the shield I need on my journey, Your unfailing love is my inspiration to rejoice in Your goodness on the earth.

*From heaven the Lord looks down and sees all mankind; from his dwelling place he watches all who live on earth—he who forms the hearts of all, who considers everything they do. No king is saved by the size of his army; no warrior escapes by his great strength. A horse is a vain hope for deliverance; despite all its great strength it cannot save. But the eyes of the Lord are on those who fear him, on those whose hope is in his unfailing love, to deliver them from death and keep them alive in famine. We wait in hope for the Lord; he is our help and our shield. In him our hearts rejoice, for we trust in his holy name. May your unfailing love rest upon us, O Lord, even as we put our hope in you.*

# July

PSALM 34:15–18

*The eyes of the Lord are on the righteous and his ears are attentive to their cry; the face of the Lord is against those who do evil, to cut off the memory of them from the earth. The righteous cry out, and the Lord hears them; he delivers them from all their troubles. The Lord is close to the broken-hearted and saves those who are crushed in spirit.*

Dear Lord,

Please count me as one of Your righteous ones through faith in Christ—my heart's desire is to truly, sincerely follow You. Please hear my broken-hearted cries and deliver me from this crushing heartbreak. Crushing is such an appropriate word, sometimes I feel so pressed down in my spirit it's a physical sensation in my chest making it hard to breathe. Yet when I close my eyes and cry for You, thankfully I feel Your gentle presence and I am able to breathe again. Keep me from doing wrong when blinded by my pain; help me to remember You are always close, always listening for me to ask for Your saving grace.

# July

# 5

Dear Lord,

How I need great peace! It is so hard not to fret, to refrain from what I feel is justifiable anger. But I do not want to inadvertently harm others nor myself by giving in to wrath; please help me be still before You, patiently waiting for the peace that passes understanding. Then when others succeed in their wicked ways, though my way continues to challenge my faith, I will honor you with my behavior and have unshakeable confidence in my eternal inheritance through my Savior Jesus Christ.

## PSALM 37:7–11

*Be still before the Lord and wait patiently for him; do not fret when men succeed in their ways, when they carry out their wicked schemes. Refrain from anger and turn from wrath; do not fret—it leads only to evil. For evil men will be cut off, but those who hope in the Lord will inherit the land. A little while, and the wicked will be no more; though you look for them, they will not be found. But the meek will inherit the land and enjoy great peace.*

# July

# 6

### PSALM 52:8–9

*But I am like an olive tree flourishing in the house of God; I trust in God's unfailing love for ever and ever. I will praise you forever for what you have done; in your name I will hope, for your name is good. I will praise you in the presence of your saints.*

Dear Lord,

Help my spirit flourish in Your presence. Thank you for Your unfailing love for me, no matter my imperfections. You see the intent of my heart of hearts is to love and serve You. I praise You that I can trust and hope in You no matter how happy or how dismal my circumstances. You lead me down the righteous path where I can honor You in all that I do. You provide all my needs, and bless me daily with Your presence. Dear God, You are so good to me.

# July

# 7

Dear Lord,

You allow us to be tested, You allow burdensome adversity in our lives, even to the point of imprisonment, literally or figuratively. Why? To refine our faith like precious metal, made stronger and purer by the fire of trials and the water of redemption. Help me understand the purpose of adversities, keep my feet from slipping while tested. May I continue to fulfill my vow of faith and trust in You when trouble has the upper hand, knowing that my life and purpose is safely in the palm of Your hand.

## PSALM 66:8–14

*Praise our God, O peoples, let the sound of his praise be heard; he has preserved our lives and kept our feet from slipping. For you, O God, tested us; you refined us like silver. You brought us into prison and laid burdens on our backs. You let men ride over our heads; we went through fire and water, but you brought us to a place of abundance. I will come to your temple with burnt offerings and fulfill my vows to you—vows my lips promised and my mouth spoke when I was in trouble.*

# July

# 8

PSALM 68:19–20, 35

*Praise be to the Lord, to God our Savior, who daily bears our burdens. Our God is a God who saves; from the Sovereign Lord comes escape from death ... You are awesome, O God, in your sanctuary; the God of Israel gives power and strength to his people. Praise be to God!*

Dear Lord,

It is such a blessing to know I do not have to bear my burdens alone. I can talk to You about them continually throughout the day and night, saving me from succumbing to my deepest, darkest fears. Your Holy Spirit provides a quiet sanctuary deep within my soul, where I can draw strength from Your constant presence, ensuring I will persevere as I praise You.

# July

## 9

### PSALM 71:5–8

Dear Lord,

I have relied on You from birth, I have always felt Your Presence in my life. I have praised You for the blessings, prayed for mercy and endurance through the tribulations. My confidence, shaky though it may be at times, is always strongly anchored in You. I do not know that I will handle the unknown well when it looms before me, but I do know that you are my refuge and comforter when I need strength and renewal to meet the challenges. May others see how You work in my life, and foretell what You will do for them as well when they hope in You. I will praise You all the days of my life, for You are my Help.

*For you have been my hope, O Sovereign Lord, my confidence since my youth. From birth I have relied on you; you brought me forth from my mother's womb. I will ever praise you. I have become like a portent to many, but you are my strong refuge. My mouth is filled with your praise, declaring your splendor all the day long.*

# July

# 10

## PSALM 71:9–16

*Do not cast me away when I am old; do not forsake me when my strength is gone. For my enemies speak against me; those who wait to kill me conspire together. They say, "God has forsaken him; pursue him and seize him, for no one will rescue him." Be not far from me, O God; come quickly, O my God, to help me. May my accusers perish in shame; may those who want to harm me be covered with scorn and disgrace. But as for me, I will always have hope; I will praise you more and more. My mouth will tell of your righteousness, of your salvation all day long, though I know not its measure. I will come and proclaim your mighty acts, O Sovereign Lord; I will proclaim your righteousness, yours alone.*

Dear Lord,

How can I always have hope when I struggle to make it through just one more minute, feeling so weighed down by heavy despair within my spirit, I feel the devil attacking my very will to breathe. When it appears You have forsaken me, that You cannot rescue me, my faith, which has been tested time and time again, reminds me how You have delivered me every single time in the past; my present and future is no different. You have not cast me away, even if I cannot feel You, You are there by my side. I will continue to hope for better days because I do not know the measure of Your greatness—it reaches beyond my trials and outlasts my despair, for in You alone is my eternal salvation and deliverance from all sorrow. I will always praise You in all circumstances.

Dear Lord,

Your law is written on my heart; I pray for relief from my days of trouble. It seems anxiety is an ever present threat to my stability, lurking in the shadows of my heart, waiting for life's cares to wear me down enough to attack. When under attack, I am ineffective to rise against wickedness in the ever raging spiritual war for souls; my feet slip, losing ground from weariness and despair. If not for Your light of salvation within my soul, in the worst heat of battle I would have gladly welcomed the peace of death as an escape—but the indwelling of Your Holy Spirit upholds me, telling me it is not for me to choose when my work here is done. Your consolation gives me courage to continue on life's journey, blessed by Your eternal love and strengthening support of Your Word.

# July

# 11

## PSALM 94:12–19

*Blessed is the man you discipline, O Lord, the man you teach from your law; you grant him relief from days of trouble, till a pit is dug for the wicked. For the Lord will not reject his people; he will never forsake his inheritance. Judgment will again be founded on righteousness, and all the upright in heart will follow it. Who will rise up for me against the wicked? Who will take a stand for me against evildoers? Unless the Lord had given me help, I would soon have dwelt in the silence of death. When I said, "My foot is slipping," your love, O Lord, supported me. When anxiety was great within me, Your consolation brought joy to my soul.*

# July

# 12

## PSALM 116:7–14

*Be at rest once more, O my soul, for the Lord has been good to you. For you, O Lord, have delivered my soul from death, my eyes from tears, my feet from stumbling, that I may walk before the Lord in the land of the living. I believed; therefore I said, "I am greatly afflicted." And in my dismay I said, "All men are liars." How can I repay the Lord for all his goodness to me? I will lift up the cup of salvation and call on the name of the Lord. I will fulfill my vows to the Lord in the presence of all his people.*

Dear Lord,

I thank you for the countless times You have comforted me through my tears; for the times You have held me up as I have stumbled along the pilgrim's way; for the times You have given me rest—spiritually, emotionally, physically. You truly have been good to me, how can I repay You? Continue, I pray, helping me live a life that honors You. Empower me to keep my vow of serving You, lead me through life for your purposes, however simple or hard. Keep me always conscious of the need for others to see You living in me, demonstrating how humbly we need to accept the cup of salvation offered through Your mercy and grace.

# July

# 13

Dear Lord,

Sometimes it is hard for me to discern when I am longing for worthless things. I strive to persevere in my faith and obedience to You when I do not understand why my hopes are unfulfilled; hopes that are not contrary to Your Word, but go unanswered for years and years. Despite my discouragement and sorrow, teach me to keep Your ways to the end; for in the end, I will ultimately find delightful peace in knowing my heart has followed You throughout my life rather than followed my own selfish gain.

## PSALM 119:33–37

*Teach me, O Lord, to follow your decrees; then I will keep them to the end. Give me understanding, and I will keep your law and obey it with all my heart. Direct me in the path of your commands, for there I find delight. Turn my heart toward your statutes and not toward selfish gain. Turn my eyes away from worthless things; preserve my life according to your word.*

# July

# 14

## PSALM 145:15–21

*The eyes of all look to you, and you give them their food at the proper time. You open your hand and satisfy the desires of every living thing. The Lord is righteous in all his ways and loving towards all he has made. The Lord is near to all who call on him, to all who call on him in truth. He fulfills the desires of those who fear him; he hears their cry and saves them. The Lord watches over all who love him, but all the wicked he will destroy. My mouth will speak in praise of the Lord. Let every creature praise his holy name forever and ever.*

Dear Lord,

Thank you for providing practical needs, food, clothing, shelter. Dear Lord, I pray You will satisfy my other desires as well, my desires for love, peace and safety. I call to You for the right direction for future hopes, desiring fulfillment from Your hand, not my own since I can be misled. Though Your way may be more difficult, I know Your way of righteousness is for the protection of my soul. When I feel destroyed by the world, remind me it is temporary; for because I praise Your name, because Your truth dwells within me, the day will come when the troubles of this world are gone, and I will forever be in Your presence, worshiping You for eternity.

# July

# 15

Dear Lord,

Heal my broken heart I pray. It aches to my very soul. Yet I am such a small being in this Universe; how can I hope You even know I exist? Because Your Word says You know the number of all the stars, surely You know all of Your created beings. Surely You know the agony my heart suffers. With Your limitless understanding, minister to my painful wounds, heal my brokenness. Gather me to Yourself, restore my soul. While I await Your comforting Presence, my spirit sings Your praise because I know my deliverance is near. And then, as I praise and worship You, Your power washes over my grateful heart, granting my longing for relief.

## PSALM 147:1–7

*Praise the Lord. How good it is to sing praises to our God, how pleasant and fitting to praise him! The Lord builds up Jerusalem; he gathers the exiles of Israel. He heals the brokenhearted and binds up their wounds. He determines the number of the stars and calls them each by name. Great is our Lord and mighty in power; his understanding has no limit. The Lord sustains the humble but casts the wicked to the ground. Sing to the Lord with thanksgiving; make music to our God on the harp.*

# July

# 16

## EXODUS 14:13–14, 29–31

*Moses answered the people, "Do not be afraid. Stand firm and you will see the deliverance the Lord will bring you today. The Egyptians you see today you will never see again. The Lord will fight for you; you need only to be still." ... But the Israelites went through the sea on dry ground, with a wall of water on their right and on their left. That day the Lord saved Israel from the hands of the Egyptians, and Israel saw the Egyptians lying dead on the shore. And when the Israelites saw the great power the Lord displayed against the Egyptians, the people feared the Lord and put their trust in him and in Moses his servant.*

Dear Lord,

Help me stand firm until Your deliverance. I feel imprisoned by my situation, just as the Israelites were enslaved in Egypt. Help me remember You are on my side. You are fighting the battle for me and I need only be still, listening carefully for Your orders. And as I obey, I trust You will deliver me.

# July

# 17

Dear Lord,

Thank you for Your voice, the Holy Spirit, which guides me every day in Your way. In Old Testament days your people needed prophets like Moses to tell them what You said. However, keeping the Law proved too hard for man, so You sent Your Son Jesus who brought mercy and grace to us. He left the Holy Spirit here on earth to dwell in each one of us individually; we don't have to wait for someone else to tell us about God's will. I prayerfully read Your Word for myself, and Your Holy Spirit helps me understand it. When I am tested, stop me from grumbling that life isn't going my way; rather help me pay attention to the prompting of the Holy Spirit, trusting in Your provision and direction.

## EXODUS 15:23–26

*When they came to Marah, they could not drink its water because it was bitter. (That is why the place is called Marah.) So the people grumbled against Moses, saying, "What are we to drink?" Then Moses cried out to the Lord, and the Lord showed him a piece of wood. He threw it into the water, and the water became sweet. There the Lord made a decree and a law for them, and there he tested them. He said, "If you listen carefully to the voice of the Lord your God and do what is right in his eyes, if you pay attention to his commands and keep all his decrees, I will not bring on you any of the diseases I brought on the Egyptians, for I am the Lord, who heals you."*

# July

# 18

## DEUTERONOMY 13:3B–4

*The Lord your God is testing you to find out whether you love him with all your heart and with all your soul. It is the Lord your God you must follow, and him you must revere. Keep his commands and obey him; serve him and hold fast to him.*

Dear Lord,

Your tests can be long and hard. How many do I have to pass before I prove I love You with all my heart and soul? I follow You, I revere You, I try hard to obey Your commands; when I stumble, I repent, and continue serving You with my whole heart. Your Holy Spirit reminds me Your truth is everlasting, whereas the tests are temporary. Passing each one means I chose You over Satan the deceiver, who wants me to give up when I perceive tests are too hard so I will ultimately perish. Instead, I will continue facing each test, each earthly challenge, holding fast to Your commands and truth.

# July

# 19

### DEUTERONOMY
### 32:3–4

*I will proclaim the name of the Lord. Oh, praise the greatness of our God! He is the Rock, his works are perfect, and all his ways are just. A faithful God who does no wrong, upright and just is he.*

Dear Lord,

You are my Rock. Observing the incredible intricacies of outer space, of this earth, of plants and animals and man, I know Your works are perfectly designed, though they may be tainted by worldly interference. Despite when circumstances seem to be contrary, I know You are just and faithful. I will proclaim Your greatness, and praise You all my days.

# July

# 20

### JOSHUA 23:14–16

*"Now I am about to go the way of all the earth. You know with all your heart and soul that not one of all the good promises the Lord your God gave you has failed. Every promise has been fulfilled; not one has failed. But just as every good promise of the Lord your God has come true, so the Lord will bring on you all the evil he has threatened, until he has destroyed you from this good land he has given you. If you violate the covenant of the Lord your God, which he commanded you, and go and serve other gods and bow down to them, the Lord's anger will burn against you, and you will quickly perish from the good land he has given you."*

Dear Lord,

Thank You that I may know without a doubt You are Lord; that Your promises are true and without fail. The good promises for believers and judgment promises for those who bow down to other gods. May Your Word live in me so I do not violate my covenant with You—to love You with all my heart, all my soul, and all my mind. I pray for discernment when other things threaten to harm my relationship with You; it is to You and You alone my spirit bows down in worship and praise.

# July

# 21

Dear Lord,

Who am I, that you would be interested in me and my family's welfare? David was a King, chosen by You. If he felt unworthy, so much more do I, since I am of little consequence to the world. Yet You promise good things to Your servants; who I am, in You, is of great consequence. You have brought me a great distance through this world, and I pray I will always follow Your lead, proving to be a trustworthy and reliable servant. I pray Your blessing upon my family and my home; and I pray I will be a blessing to those I come in contact with as I go about my day.

## II SAMUEL 7:18–19, 28–29

*Then King David went in and sat before the Lord, and he said: "Who am I, O Sovereign Lord, and what is my family, that you have brought me this far? And as if this were not enough in your sight, O Sovereign Lord, you have also spoken about the future of the house of your servant. Is this your usual way of dealing with man, O Sovereign Lord?" ... "O Sovereign Lord, you are God! Your words are trustworthy, and you have promised these good things to your servant. Now be pleased to bless the house of your servant, that it may continue forever in your sight; for you, O Sovereign Lord, have spoken, and with your blessing the house of your servant will be blessed forever."*

# July

# 22

## I CHRONICLES 22:12–14A

*"May the Lord give you discretion and understanding when he puts you in command over Israel, so that you may keep the law of the Lord your God. Then you will have success if you are careful to observe the decrees and laws that the Lord gave to Moses for Israel. Be strong and courageous. Do not be afraid or discouraged. I have taken great pains to provide for the temple of the Lord ... "*

Dear Lord,

Just as You gave King David discretion and understanding to command the nation of Israel, I pray you will help me command what You place within my control: my spiritual growth, my choices, my attitude, my family, my work ethic. Help me not be afraid or discouraged but know that You have taken great pains to provide for me through Your Son Jesus Christ.

# July

# 23

Dear Lord,

Thank you that the promises You made thousands of years ago to King David are still kept today. Help me keep the promises I voice with my mouth by practical action with my hands, using my time, money and talent to serve You wholeheartedly.

## II CHRONICLES 6:14–15

*He said: "O Lord, God of Israel, there is no God like you in heaven or on earth—you who keep your covenant of love with your servants who continue wholeheartedly in your way. You have kept your promise to your servant David my father; with your mouth you have promised and with your hand you have fulfilled it—as it is today."*

# July

# 24

### JOB 5:17–19

*"Blessed is the man whom God corrects; so do not despise the discipline of the Almighty. For he wounds, but he also binds up; he injures, but his hands also heal. From six calamities he will rescue you; in seven no harm will befall you.*

Dear Lord,

Help me discern Your discipline is different from man's discipline—that Yours is discipleship rather than punishment. Your corrections, Your wounds, Your injuries are the sculpting process; You mold my spirit into conformity with Your image. The calamity would be if the clay of my heart was too hardened to yield under Your firm, loving touch.

# July

# 25

## JOB 13:15

*Though he slay me, yet will I hope in him.*

## PROVERBS 23:17–18

*Do not let your heart envy sinners, but always be zealous for the fear of the Lord. There is surely a future hope for you, and your hope will not be cut off.*

Dear Lord,

Help me trust You no matter the circumstances. Sometimes it feels like You do not hear me, that You will not help me when I need it so badly. However, I want to be like Job—though You slay me, I still know I am in Your care. Those lost in sin do not know their hope is cut off; those who do not believe in You are destined for eternal torture—I know it's true. I fear You, not in the sense of being afraid, rather out of reverential awe for Your Deity, Your Power, Your Wrath towards sin. I pray for those whose souls wait for their minds and hearts to be drawn to You.

# July

# 26

## JOB 42:1–3

*Then Job replied to the Lord: "I know that you can do all things; no plan of yours can be thwarted. You asked 'Who is this that obscures my counsel without knowledge?' Surely I spoke of things I did not understand, things too wonderful for me to know."*

Dear Lord,

Help me so I do not obscure Your counsel. Help me seek knowledge tempered with Your wisdom so I do not thwart Your will—through misunderstanding, misguided thinking, or especially not out of deliberate disobedience. I sincerely pray You help me hold in deepest regard Your Holy Word, for I know You can do all things, things too wonderful for me to know.

# July

# 27

Dear Lord,

In many ways this world is loveless and faithless—help me keep love and faith strong in my heart. Even when I do not understand the why, what, where or when of things, help me still trust in the Who— God the Father, God the Son, and God the Holy Spirit. Engrave Your Word into the tablet of my heart so that it will never leave me, it will testify to Your constant presence in my life, as I do my best to acknowledge You in all my ways. Thank you for guiding my path.

## PROVERBS 3:3–6

*Let love and faithfulness never leave you; bind them around your neck, write them on the tablet of your heart. Then you will find favor and a good name in the sight of God and man. Trust in the Lord with all your heart and lean not on your own understanding; in all your ways acknowledge him, and he will make your paths straight.*

# July

# 28

## PROVERBS
3:9–12

*Honor the Lord with your wealth, with the first fruits of all your crops; then your barns will be filled to overflowing, and your vats will brim over with new wine. My son, do not despise the Lord's discipline and do not resent his rebuke, because the Lord disciplines those he loves, as a father the son he delights in.*

Dear Lord,

I need help honoring You with my wealth, because I do not feel wealthy—I feel barely able to provide for my family. Yet we manage to have food, clothing and shelter each day; so You are faithful in sharing Your wealth of provision with us. Help me remember, as You sometimes chasten me about properly sharing back to Your kingdom from my resources, however limited they may be, that this discipline means You are discipling me to grow and show others how to live life trusting in Your ways.

# July

# 29

## PROVERBS
4:4–5, 13–14

*… he taught me and said, "Lay hold of my words with all your heart; keep my commands and you will live. Get wisdom, get understanding; do not forget my words or swerve from them … Hold on to instruction, do not let it go; guard it well, for it is your life. Do not set foot on the path of the wicked or walk in the way of evil men.*

Dear Lord,

Thank you for the hunger in my soul to lay hold of Your Words. I pray You grow wisdom and understanding in my heart, and may I never forget to let Your instruction temper my proactive and reactive responses to life situations. Guard my heart, keep me from disobedience. I am determined to honor and obey the Way, the Truth, and the Life, which is in Christ Jesus.

# July

# 30

## PROVERBS
21;2–3, 23

*All a man's ways seem right to him, but the Lord weighs the heart. To do what is right and just is more acceptable to the Lord than sacrifice ... He who guards his mouth and his tongue keeps himself from calamity.*

Dear Lord,

Guard my heart, mind and soul I pray. May I always make Your Spirit the strongest influence in my life. Weigh what I think is right; warn me if it is not, so I will not bring calamity on others nor myself. Rather than congratulate myself for giving up or sacrificing something I want, keep my motives pure, wanting only to do what is right and just before the Lord because this is Your desire for Your people.

# July

# 31

### PROVERBS
22:1–2, 23:4–5

Dear Lord,

In my quest to earn money, it is truly not my intention to gain riches; it is to provide adequately for my children. Meeting our needs wears me out, I pray for Your strength. I pray for Your Wisdom on managing finances, providing for my family physically, emotionally, and spiritually. It is through spiritual provision that we grow a good name, earning esteem from others through following God. I pray I grow a family with a good name, and it is our spirits rather than temporal riches that soar as eagles.

*A good name is more desirable than great riches; to be esteemed is better than silver or gold. Rich and poor have this in common: The Lord is the Maker of them all ... Do not wear yourself out to get rich; have the wisdom to show restraint. Cast but a glance at riches, and they are gone, for they will surely sprout wings and fly off to the sky like an eagle.*

# August

## 1

### PROVERBS 30:7–9

*"Two things I ask of you, O Lord; do not refuse me before I die: Keep falsehood and lies far from me; give me neither poverty nor riches, but give me only my daily bread. Otherwise, I may have too much and disown you and say, 'Who is the Lord?' Or I may become poor and steal, and so dishonor the name of my God.*

Dear Lord,

I ask for Your strength to keep me from falsehoods and lies—thank You for instilling Your truths into my nature so I am uncomfortable with such things. I too ask for enough to provide for my family and I; for food, shelter and clothing, and just enough for a few wants to give us blessings, but not enough to encourage selfish expectations. Should You provide us with much, may we be likewise generous with much to others. When we have only a little, may we be grateful You stretch it to be enough.

# August

## 2

Dear Lord,

My toil gets overwhelming sometimes, and I have to wonder what is it all for? What do I gain? Why do You allow such a burden to challenge me to the core of my being? I see—to make sure You are at my core—to make sure I consider what I do in light of eternity. And that is my heart's desire: to be centered on Christ. Help me be happy despite the toil, and to always honor You by doing good.

### ECCLESIASTES 3:9–14

*What does the worker gain from his toil? I have seen the burden God has laid on men. He has made everything beautiful in its time. He has also set eternity in the hearts of men; yet they cannot fathom what God has done from beginning to end. I know that there is nothing better for men than to be happy and do good while they live. That everyone may eat and drink, and find satisfaction in all his toil— this is the gift of God. I know that everything God does will endure forever; nothing can be added to it and nothing taken from it. God does it so that men will revere him.*

# August

# 3

## ECCLESIASTES
5:18

*Then I realized that it is good and proper for a man to eat and drink, and to find satisfaction in his toilsome labor under the sun during the few days of life God has given him—for this is his lot.*

Dear Lord,

There are times my toil seems so tiresome, the tasks set before me are too great. Yet I must press on, struggling to provide even the very basics for my family: food, clothing and shelter. Help me accept my lot in life, finding satisfaction in both the trying and the triumphing in the tasks You set before me, knowing that whether they be menial or magnificent, they are what You have asked me to do. And I want to do them well and willingly to please you.

# August

### ECCLESIASTES 9:11–12

*I have seen something else under the sun: The race is not to the swift or the battle to the strong, nor does food come to the wise or wealth to the brilliant or favor to the learned; but time and chance happen to them all. Moreover, no man knows when his hour will come: As fish are caught in a cruel net, or birds taken in a snare, so men are trapped by evil times that fall unexpectedly upon them.*

Dear Lord,

I am taught to pray, to seek Your will, Your guidance, Your protection. Then I make decisions, and despite my best efforts, the worst happens. Thank you for scriptures that tell me it is not necessarily that I was wrong, or misinterpreted Your answer, or I am being punished, or You don't care. Rather it is because I live in this imperfect world, time and chance will happen for better or worse. Help me remember for better or worse, You are always beside me to walk me through.

# August

# 5

### ISAIAH 6:8, 7:9B

*Then I heard the voice of the Lord saying, "Whom shall I send? And who will go for us?" And I said, "Here am I. Send me!" … "If you do not stand firm in your faith, you will not stand at all."*

Dear Lord,

I am willing with all my heart, soul, and mind to be Your servant; to do what You want me to do, be what You want me to be, and to say what You want me to say. I am here for You—I pray You will be my strength when I find the road You send me on is too difficult. With Your everlasting arms to lean on, I will be able to stand firm.

# August

# 6

Dear Lord,

When my life feels out of my control, when things don't seem to go the way I need them to go for my family and my sake, when I am just too overwhelmed by the yoke I am under, please help me remember this scripture. "Surely as I have planned it so it will be." You have a purpose for everything that happens in our lives, and as I trust in You, Your plan for me and my house cannot be thwarted. Thank you Lord!

## ISAIAH 14:24–27

*The Lord Almighty has sworn, "Surely, as I have planned, so it will be, and as I have purposed, so it will stand. I will crush the Assyrian in my land; on my mountains I will trample him down. His yoke will be taken from my people, and his burden removed from their shoulders." This is the plan determined for the whole world; this is the hand stretched out over all nations. For the Lord Almighty has purposed, and who can thwart him? His hand is stretched out, and who can turn it back?*

# August

# 7

## ISAIAH 25:1, 26:3–4,12

*O Lord, you are my God; I will exalt you and praise your name, for in perfect faithfulness you have done marvelous things, things planned long ago ... You will keep in perfect peace him whose mind is steadfast, because he trusts in you. Trust in the Lord forever, for the Lord, the Lord, is the Rock eternal ... Lord, you establish peace for us; all that we have accomplished you have done for us.*

Dear Lord,

Thank you for Your perfect faithfulness to me. Even though I fail You, You never fail me. When my world trembles, I struggle with the initial reaction to worry or panic; then I do my best to change my fretful reactions to actions in prayer and worship for my Rock Eternal. I pursue perfect peace in You. I remind myself of all You have accomplished for me in the past; my trust remains steadfast in Your name. Help me continue to seek and follow Your plan for my life.

# August

## 8

Dear Lord,

The world is so busy and hectic, no time for quietness and rest. No matter what the clamor around me, I pray I always hear Your voice behind me saying "This is the way, walk ye in it." With Your voice behind me, help me resist temptations leading in other directions; rather I pray I always trust in Your strong spiritual prompting as it leads me forward in Your direction.

ISAIAH 30:15, 21

*This is what the Sovereign Lord, the Holy One of Israel, says: "In repentance and rest is your salvation, in quietness and trust is your strength … " Whether you turn to the right or to the left, your ears will hear a voice behind you saying, "This is the way; walk ye in it."*

# August

## 9

### ISAIAH 54:4–5

*"Do not be afraid; you will not suffer shame. Do not fear disgrace; you will not be humiliated. You will forget the shame of your youth and remember no more the reproach of your widowhood. For your Maker is your husband—the Lord Almighty is his name—the Holy One of Israel is your Redeemer; he is called the God of all the earth."*

Dear Lord,

I don't understand how my Maker can be my husband. A husband is a man in a marital relationship with me—it is what I want, but it has not come to pass. Desperate to understand, I read the definition of husband: the archaic meaning is manager of household, steward; to manage carefully, be saving of; make the most of ... Precious Lord, thank You for revealing to me, in my aloneness, You are my Manager, You are my Savior. In You is how I make the most of my life. This, this meaning I understand.

# August

# 10

Dear Lord,

I pray for Your comfort—I mourn broken promises, lost hopes, and ache with despair over devastated dreams. I see why the ancients grieved externally in sackcloth and ashes—beautiful dreams, burnt to the ground, end with just the soul sitting in ashes. But Your Word says You will provide for me; please plant within my heart new promises, new hopes, new truths that will be borne out of these ashes. Rebuild my spirit so it is stronger and more determined than ever to live for Your glory.

## ISAIAH 61:2B–4

*... to comfort all who mourn, and provide for those who grieve in Zion—to bestow on them a crown of beauty instead of ashes, the oil of gladness instead of mourning, and a garment of praise instead of a spirit of despair. They will be called oaks of righteousness, a planting of the Lord for the display of his splendor. They will rebuild the ancient ruins and restore the places long devastated; they will renew the ruined cities that have been devastated for generations.*

# August

## 11

### LAMENTATIONS
#### 3:17–23

*I have been deprived of peace; I have forgotten what prosperity is. So I say, "My splendor is gone and all that I had hoped from the Lord." I remembered my affliction and my wandering, the bitterness and the gall. I well remember them, and my soul is downcast within me. Yet this I call to mind and therefore I have hope: Because of the Lord's great love we are not consumed, for his compassions never fail. They are new every morning; great is your faithfulness.*

Dear Lord,

I have been deprived of peace so long. The naïve hope of my youth is long gone, replaced with the ache of broken dreams. Like the psalmist, my soul is downcast within me. I may appear to those around me to be calm and in control—only You know the chaos in my heart and mind. Yet also like the psalmist, I have experienced Your great compassion shining into my soul throughout the storm. My afflictions cannot consume me because of Your great faithful love.

# August

# 12

## LAMENTATIONS
3:24–26

Dear Lord,

You are my portion; strengthen me, I pray, so I do not lose hope when temporary trials impede my path. May I wait quietly in prayer for Your intercession and deliverance. Your grace is more than sufficient to sustain me through my ups and downs. You provide my needs spiritually, emotionally, mentally and physically. My hope is in Your eternal goodness.

*I say to myself, "The Lord is my portion; therefore I will wait for him." The Lord is good to those whose hope is in him, to the one who seeks him; it is good to wait quietly for the salvation of the Lord.*

# August

# 13

## HOSEA 6:1–6

*"Come, let us return to the Lord. He has torn us to pieces but he will heal us; he has injured us but he will bind up our wounds. After two days he will revive us; on the third day he will restore us, that we may live in his presence. Let us acknowledge the Lord; let us press on to acknowledge him. As surely as the sun rises, he will appear; he will come to us like the winter rains, like the spring rains that water the earth." "What can I do with you, Ephraim? What can I do with you, Judah? Your love is like the morning mist, like the early dew that disappears. Therefore I cut you in pieces with my prophets, I killed you with the words of my mouth; my judgments flashed like lightning upon you. For I desire mercy, not sacrifice, and acknowledgement of God rather than burnt offerings."*

Dear Lord,

The Israelites turned from You to their own ways, as we do today. Now, as then, You allow us to be torn up, injured by the consequences of our own poor choices, and then we blame You for it. It should not be—I need to acknowledge You in all that I do, every day, and press on to know You more. Then, as the rain nourishes the earth, Your Word nourishes my soul in the ways to avoid the perils of sin. I pray my public devotion is not like a morning mist, disappearing in the heat of another's scrutiny because I am afraid of their judgment. Rather I need to fear Your judgment, respect Your Sovereignty. Further, stop me from being self-righteous and judging others; You show me mercy when I return to You; I must do no less, following Your example of compassion for my fellow man.

# August

## 14

Dear Lord,

As the prophet, I dread future trouble. Yet, I must wait patiently for the day all my fears are conquered, regardless of the circumstances. Even though, like the prophet says, the things I need to live, such as money for food, shelter, clothing, is sparse, I can still rejoice in the Lord. I am never out of Your sight. You know my needs and hopes and dreams. Align them with Your plan; grow the fruit of Your Spirit in me: love, joy, peace, patience, kindness, goodness, faithfulness, gentleness and self-control. With Your guidance I have a sure foothold on the mountains of life, and I will reach the heights of victory with Your strength.

## HABAKKUK 3:16–19

*I heard and my heart pounded, my lips quivered at the sound; decay crept into my bones, and my legs trembled. Yet I will wait patiently for the day of calamity to come on the nation invading us. Though the fig tree does not bud and there are no grapes on the vine, though the olive crop fails and the fields produce no food, though there are no sheep in the pen and no cattle in the stalls, yet I will rejoice in the Lord, I will be joyful in God my Savior. The Sovereign Lord is my strength; he makes my feet like the feet of a deer, he enables me to go on the heights.*

# August

# 15

## ZECHARIAH 4:6–10A

*So he said to me, "This is the word of the Lord to Zerubbabel: 'Not by might nor by power, but by my Spirit,' says the Lord Almighty. "What are you, O mighty mountain? Before Zerubbabel you will become level ground. Then he will bring out the capstone to shouts of 'God bless it! God bless it!'" Then the word of the Lord came to me: "The hands of Zerubbabel have laid the foundation of this temple; his hands will also complete it. Then you will know that the Lord Almighty has sent me to you. Who despises the day of small things? Men will rejoice when they see the plumb line in the hand of Zerubbabel."*

Dear Lord,

Thank you for the examples in the Old Testament where You interceded on behalf of Your people. Your Word tells me it is not by my might nor by my power, but by Your Spirit the victory is won, I need not fear. Though I feel overwhelmed, insurmountable obstacles are laid waste in the face of Your Will. You are the cornerstone and the capstone of my existence; the foundation of my faith and the completion of my soul is found only with You. You are in the small things, and the big things that I experience; You are the plumb line, my center of gravity, in You my world holds together. Just as it was in Zerubbabel's day, the Lord Almighty is in control of man's destiny; I accept Your Lordship of my life, and I pray I daily surrender to Your will.

# August

## 16

Dear Lord,

In this day of modern technology many have their confidence in man's knowledge rather than in God's Wisdom. Ancient religious truths are easily dismissed as myths; stories told to explain the unknown. The word 'righteousness' is outdated, let alone properly understood in the context of our time. While I do not feel particularly blessed when I am insulted for believing in You, I pray You will empower me to risk insults, if need be, because I must remain true to following Your Righteousness. I believe my ultimate reward awaits in the eternity of heaven with You.

### MATTHEW 5:10–12

*Blessed are those who are persecuted because of righteousness, for theirs is the kingdom of heaven. Blessed are you when people insult you, persecute you and falsely say all kinds of evil against you because of me. Rejoice and be glad, because great is your reward in heaven, for in the same way they persecuted the prophets who were before you.*

# August

# 17

## MATTHEW 11:25–30

*At that time Jesus said, "I praise you, Father, Lord of heaven and earth, because you have hidden these things from the wise and learned, and revealed them to children. Yes, Father, for this was your good pleasure. All things have been committed to me by my Father. No one knows the Son except the Father, and no one knows the Father except the Son and those to whom the Son chooses to reveal him. Come to me, all you who are weary and burdened, and I will give you rest. Take my yoke upon you and learn of me, for I am gentle and humble in heart, and you will find rest for your souls. For my yoke is easy and my burden is light."*

Dear Lord,

Rest? Goodness, how I need rest! For my mind, body and soul! Lord, there is much I do not understand. I come to You humbly, as a child, not seeking God's wisdom through worldly knowledge, rather through the ministry of the Godhead: Father, Son and Holy Spirit. Reveal to me how to release my cares to You; show me that taking on Your yoke, giving You the reigns to guide me, will make my burdens lighter and give me rest as You lead me through the troubled waters.

# August

# 18

Dear Lord,

I pray with all my heart I never become one who is 'ever hearing, but never understanding, ever seeing, but never perceiving.' Open wide my eyes, my Lord, that I may see all there is to do for You. Speak in whatever ways I need to hear You so I may understand the tasks set before me. Live in my heart, that I may always be blessed with Your presence as I am about Your plan for my life.

## MATTHEW 13:13–16

*This is why I speak to them in parables: "Though seeing, they do not see; though hearing, they do not hear or understand." In them is fulfilled the prophecy of Isaiah: "You will be ever hearing but never understanding; you will be ever seeing but never perceiving. For this people's heart has become calloused; they hardly hear with their ears, and they have closed their eyes. Otherwise they might see with their eyes, hear with their ears, understand with their hearts and turn, and I would heal them." But blessed are your eyes because they see, and your ears because they hear.*

# August

# 19

## MATTHEW 16:24–27

*Then Jesus said to his disciples, "If anyone would come after me, he must deny himself and take up his cross and follow me. For whoever wants to save his life will lose it, but whoever loses his life for me will find it. What good will it be for a man if he gains the whole world, yet forfeits his soul? Or what can a man give in exchange for his soul? For the Son of Man is going to come in his Father's glory with his angels, and then he will reward each person according to what he has done [practiced]."*

Dear Lord,

May it be my practice to take up my cross daily to follow after You. When it's hard to trust troubles will become small compared to the whole of Your plan for my life, let me remember Your Sacrifice, Your Triumph over the world through the work of the Cross. May I lose my life in You, not in worldly cares. As Your Word says, I have nothing to exchange for my soul; I gain salvation only through Your Mercy and Grace.

# August
# 20

Dear Lord,

My faith grows weak when my prayers go unanswered, when the mountain of difficulty remains before me instead of falling into the sea of victory. Did I not pray right, claiming victory before the battle is won? Am I not following Your direction; do I need to re-direct my steps, is that the reason why this prayer is still unanswered? Is the desire in my heart not in Your plan? Or maybe I have not adequately forgiven those who have hurt me? So many questions when hope is fading. I pray forgiveness for my weakness, and mercy as I ask for guidance. Closing my eyes, I recall how many times You have answered prayer in the past, and am strengthened by Your faithfulness. And when I open my eyes, the mountain does not look so tall.

## MARK 11:22–26

*"Have faith in God," Jesus answered. "I tell you the truth, if anyone says to this mountain, 'Go, throw yourself into the sea,' and does not doubt in his heart but believes that what he says will happen, it will be done for him. Therefore I tell you, whatever you ask for in prayer, believe that you have received it and it will be yours. And when you stand praying, if you hold anything against anyone, forgive him, so that your Father in heaven may forgive you your sins."*

# August

# 21

## LUKE 17:5–10

*The apostles said to the Lord, "Increase our faith!" He replied, "If you have faith as small as a mustard seed, you can say to this mulberry tree, 'Be uprooted and planted in the sea,' and it will obey you. Suppose one of you had a servant plowing or looking after sheep. Would he say to the servant when he comes in from the field, 'Come along now and sit down to eat?' Would he not rather say, 'Prepare my supper, get yourself ready and wait on me while I eat and drink; after that you may eat and drink?' Would he thank the servant because he did what he was told to do? So you also, when you have done everything you were told to do, should say, 'We are unworthy servants; we have only done our duty.'"*

Dear Lord,

Should I boast in good deeds I have done, quickly remind me it is You who makes all things possible. True knowledge and wisdom come from You alone. May I give You the glory for everything, remembering I am an unworthy servant, covered by the blood of the Lamb. When serving You is hard to do, increase my faith from the size of a mustard seed so I may do what You require of me, whether it is possible or seemingly impossible by man's standards.

# August

# 22

Dear Lord,

Thank you that Your Word covers so many things that cannot separate us from Your love. Through Your love, I pray that You will not let anything within me separate me from You or Your commands—my insecurities, my doubts, my failures, my weaknesses, my depression, my pain, my brokenness. May Your Spirit be ever-present in my life to gently and firmly draw me back when I go astray. I am convinced that I am more than a conqueror through my Lord Jesus Christ!

## ROMANS 8:35–39

*Who shall separate us from the love of Christ? Shall trouble or hardship or persecution or famine or nakedness or danger or sword? As it is written: "For your sake we face death all day long; we are considered as sheep to be slaughtered." No, in all these things we are more than conquerors through him who loved us. For I am convinced that neither death nor life, neither angel nor demons, neither the present nor the future, nor any powers, neither height nor depth, nor anything else in all creation, will be able to separate us from the love of God that is in Christ Jesus our Lord.*

# August

# 23

## ROMANS 9:15–21

*For he says to Moses, "I will have mercy on whom I have mercy, and I will have compassion on whom I have compassion." It does not, therefore, depend on man's desire or effort, but on God's mercy. For the Scripture says to Pharaoh: "I raised you up for this very purpose, that I might display my power in you and that my name might be proclaimed in all the earth." Therefore God has mercy on whom he wants to have mercy, and he hardens whom he wants to harden. One of you will say to me: "Then why does God still blame us? For who resists his will?" But who are you, O man, to talk back to God? "Shall what is formed say to him who formed it, 'Why did you make me like this?'" Does not the potter have the right to make out of the same lump of clay some pottery for noble purposes and some for common use?*

Dear Lord,

I am guilty of this, asking You why did You make me this way. Why do I struggle daily with emotional pain, why can I not be free of aloneness, constant physical pain, financial stress? Rather, why can I not accept my lot in life and rejoice anyway since I know You are with me through it all? Forgive me Lord— may I accept the use for which you have made me, noble or common. Thank you for having mercy on me; I pray Your purpose be done in my life. Lead the way and may I serve you well, as the song says, just as I am.

# August

# 24

Dear Lord,

As I continue to build my life, may every aspect—private, social, professional—be congruent with my foundation: Jesus Christ. You, Lord, are my Cornerstone; when my life comes under fire, ready me to stand firm, prevent me from changing my building materials from what You have chosen for me. Rather let my choices show the quality of Your workmanship, evidence of prayerfully seeking Your Counsel. I want to remain safely on Your path for me, not barely saved from the fringes of sin's dangerous fire along an alternate, poorly chosen path.

## I CORINTHIANS 3:10–15

*By the grace God has given me, I laid a foundation as a wise builder, and someone else is building on it. But each one should be careful how he builds. For no one can lay any foundation other than the one already laid, which is Jesus Christ. If any man builds on this foundation using gold, silver, costly stones, wood, hay or straw, his work will be shown for what it is, because the Day will bring it to light. It will be revealed with fire, and the fire will test the quality of each man's work. If what he has built survives, he will receive his reward. If it is burned up, he will suffer loss; he himself will be saved, but only as one escaping through the flames.*

# August

# 25

## I CORINTHIANS 3:16–19

*Don't you know that you yourselves are God's temple and that God's Spirit lives in you? If anyone destroys God's temple, God will destroy him; for God's temple is sacred, and you are that temple. Do not deceive yourselves. If anyone of you thinks he is wise by the standards of this age, he should become a "fool" so that he may become wise. For the wisdom of this world is foolishness in God's sight.*

Dear Lord,

Thank you for reminding me that I am your temple. Your temple is not a place people go, rather your Spirit's dwelling place is in my heart and soul; in each one of us and all of us who believe in Your Word. Thank you I feel Your Presence anywhere that I am, because You live in me, and You are always present. The world may think the comfort and strength I draw from Your unseen existence is foolishness; yet I believe Your Word. Therefore, I will be a fool so I may know Your Wisdom and daily feel Your Holy Presence.

# August

# 26

Dear Lord,

There are many times I ask why me, why do I have to endure such painful trials and tribulations. Thank you for answering me in Your Word—so I may personally know your comfort, and share it with others. If I never hurt, how can I understand what others are going through? I must show them how to grow through it with You.

## II CORINTHIANS 1:3–5

*Praise be to the God and Father of our Lord Jesus Christ, the Father of compassion and the God of all comfort, who comforts us in all our troubles, so that we can comfort those in any trouble with the comfort we ourselves have received from God. For just as the sufferings of Christ flow over into our lives, so also through Christ our comfort overflows.*

# August

# 27

## II CORINTHIANS 3:3–5

*You show that you are a letter from Christ, the result of our ministry, written not with ink but with the Spirit of the living God, not on tablets of stone but on tablets of human hearts. Such confidence as this is ours through Christ before God. Not that we are competent in ourselves to claim anything for ourselves, but our competence comes from God.*

Dear Lord,

How can I be a letter from You to the world when I feel so torn up inside? How can anyone see You in me when my troubles overwhelm my heart? Because my confidence is in You-confidence that You will see me through, you will shine through me as I trust in You. Thank You my competence is from You rather than from within myself, so people will be able to read You in my actions.

# August

# 28

## II CORINTHIANS
4:7–9

Dear Lord,

Help me acknowledge difficult challenges, but not let them drive me to utter despair and defeat. Help me recognize that hard pressed vs. crushed, perplexed vs. despair, persecuted vs. abandoned, struck down vs. destroyed, are contrasting verbs of lost battles, not of a lost War. You have overcome the world, so the final outcome is assured. Thank you.

*But we have this treasure in jars of clay to show that this all-surpassing power is from God and not from us. We are hard pressed on every side, but not crushed; perplexed, but not in despair; persecuted, but not abandoned; struck down, but not destroyed.*

# August

# 29

## II CORINTHIANS
## 5:14–17

*For Christ's love compels us, because we are convinced that one died for all, and therefore all died. And he died for all, that those who live should no longer live for themselves but for him who died for them and was raised again. So from now on we regard no one from a worldly point of view. Though we once regarded Christ in this way, we do so no longer. Therefore, if anyone is in Christ, he is a new creation; the old has gone, the new has come!*

Dear Lord,

No words can express my deepest gratitude for salvation through Your sacrifice. You lived to die for me, the ultimate and final sacrifice, so that all may have eternal life through You. Death had no hold on You, for You rose from the dead to sit again at the right hand of the Father, keeping watch over my soul. Your love compels me to live for You, as I am a new creation with You in my heart. I am forever convinced You are my Lord and Savior!

# August

# 30

## II CORINTHIANS
5:18–21

*All this is from God, who reconciles us to himself through Christ and gave us the ministry of reconciliation: that God was reconciling the world to himself in Christ, not counting men's sins against them. And he has committed to us the message of reconciliation. We are therefore Christ's ambassadors, as though God were making his appeal through us. We implore you on Christ's behalf: Be reconciled to God. God made him who had no sin to be sin for us, so that in him we might become the righteousness of God.*

Dear Lord,

Thank you for Your merciful reconciliation. If not for Christ's sacrifice, the filth of sin would forever taint my soul; I would be lost without hope of entering into Your Holy Presence, never sharing in Your righteousness. In Him, hallelujah, my sins are covered by Your grace; in honest repentance I may humbly come before You. Send me as an ambassador of Your message within the circle of my influence. Through the way I live my life, may I inspire others to be reconciled to You through Jesus Christ.

# August

# 31

## II CORINTHIANS
## 9:6–8

*Remember this: Whoever sows sparingly will also reap sparingly, and whoever sows generously will also reap generously. Each man should give what he has decided in his heart to give, not reluctantly or under compulsion, for God loves a cheerful giver. And God is able to make all grace abound to you, so that in all things at all times, having all that you need, you will abound in every good work.*

Dear Lord,

Thank you for the resources you provide, sometimes just in the nick of time, sometimes in ways I never imagined. Help me use your generosity as the example for me to be generous back towards You, not only with my time and talent, but with my resources as well. I want to be a cheerful giver, please help me, when resources are low and I fear for tomorrow, to remember my life is in Your hands. You give me my work abilities, my willingness to volunteer, the desire to give back a portion of the resources you have given me. May I always honor You with everything I have and everything I do.

# September

## 1

Dear Lord,

You had the plan of salvation for all mankind before the beginning of the world. While Old Testament spoke of the Jews as God's chosen people, the New Testament reveals You predestined Christ's salvation to be available for both Jew and Gentile alike. You freely offer spiritual blessings to any and all who will believe in Your saving grace through Jesus Christ. You chose each one of us to be holy and spiritually blameless in Your sight, which is only accomplished through the redemption found in His shed blood. I pray forgiveness for my transgressions, and that I daily grow in Your wisdom and understanding so I may be about the Lord's business all the days of my life.

### EPHESIANS 1:3–8

*Praise be to the God and Father of our Lord Jesus Christ, who has blessed us in the heavenly realms with every spiritual blessing in Christ. For he chose us in him before the creation of the world to be holy and blameless in his sight. In love he predestined us to be adopted as his sons through Jesus Christ, in accordance with his pleasure and will—to the praise of his glorious grace, which he has freely given us in the One he loves. In him we have redemption through his blood, the forgiveness of sins, in accordance with the riches of God's grace that he lavished on us with all wisdom and understanding.*

# September

# 2

## PHILIPPIANS 1:3, 6, 9–11

*I thank my God every time I remember you ... being confident of this, that he who began a good work in you will carry it on to completion until the day of Christ Jesus ... And this is my prayer: that your love may abound more and more in knowledge and depth of insight, so that you may be able to discern what is best and may be pure and blameless until the day of Christ, filled with the fruit of righteousness that comes through Jesus Christ—to the glory and praise of God.*

Dear Lord,

It is difficult to be confident when there are deceitful messages being spread all around us. My loved ones, myself, may be misled by teachings that sound right when first presented. I pray for those, including myself, in whom You began a good work that You will bring to completion in Jesus Christ on the appointed day. Along with the Biblical disciple, I pray that my love for You may abound more and more. I want to grow in knowledge and wisdom of You through Your Word. Deepen my insight to who You are within me, filling me with the fruit of Your righteousness through Jesus Christ.

# September

# 3

### PHILIPPIANS
### 1:18–19, 27

Dear Lord,

Sometimes I cannot help but question other people's motives when they do questionable things in Your Name. Are they doing it for their own glory or Yours? But here in Your Word the point is made, whether motives are false or true, if the truth of Christ is being preached, it does not matter, Your Word is being shared. Regardless of what others are doing, I am to conduct myself worthy of the gospel of Jesus Christ. My motives need always be pure—always for Your glory, regardless what is thought of me. I do not want to be the cause of anyone stumbling or falling away because they discover false motives in my actions. I look to You for keeping my motives pure.

*But what does it matter? The important thing is that in every way, whether from false motives or true, Christ is preached. And because of this I rejoice. Yes, and I will continue to rejoice, for I know that through your prayers and the help given by the Spirit of Jesus Christ, what has happened to me will turn out for my deliverance ... Whatever happens, conduct yourselves in a manner worthy of the gospel of Christ.*

# September

# 4

## COLOSSIANS
### 1:12–14

*… and giving joyful thanks to the Father, who has qualified you to share in the inheritance of the saints in the kingdom of light. For he has rescued us from the dominion of darkness and brought us into the kingdom of the Son he loves, in whom we have redemption, the forgiveness of sins.*

Dear Lord,

Along with my laundry list of needs, I try to remember to thank You daily for some small or large blessing in my life. For the ability to breathe and see, for mountains and flowers, for a monthly income on which to live, for being born in the USA, and most of all for my beloved children and family. But, really, the most precious of all is the forgiveness of sin and the eternal inheritance in the Kingdom of Heaven; I am ashamed to say it may seem I take it for granted since I have been a believer from childhood. Please know I am <u>always</u> grateful for this most precious gift, and it is why I love and serve You, my Savior.

Dear Lord,

Thank You so much for these encouraging words! I do not grieve as those who have no hope, rather because I believe Jesus died and rose again, the believer's physical death is really just falling asleep in the Lord. When You return for us, Your command will wake those asleep in You, and with those who are living, all believers will be caught up in the air to meet You in victory over death. And so shall believers ever be in Your presence from that day through eternity. So losing a saved loved one from this earthly realm is painful and feels tragic, but the truth is the separation is temporary. I will see them again in the heavenly realm, and worship with them at Your feet for Your mercy and grace. May those without hope turn to You, believe, and also be with us on that day!

# September

# 5

## I THESSALONIANS 4:13–18

*Brothers, we do not want you to be ignorant about those who fall asleep, or to grieve like the rest of men, who have no hope. We believe that Jesus died and rose again and so we believe that God will bring with Jesus those who have fallen asleep in him. According to the Lord's own word, we tell you that we who are still alive, who are left till the coming of the Lord, will certainly not precede those who have fallen asleep. For the Lord himself will come down from heaven, with a loud command, with the voice of the archangel and with the trumpet call of God, and the dead in Christ will rise first. After that, we who are still alive and are left will be caught up together with them in the clouds to meet the Lord in the air. And so we will be with the Lord forever. Therefore encourage each other with these words.*

# September

# 6

## II THESSALONIANS
## 2:15–17, 3:3–5

*So then, brothers, stand firm and hold to the teachings we passed on to you, whether by word of mouth or by letter. May our Lord Jesus Christ himself and God our Father, who loved us and by his grace gave us eternal encouragement and good hope, encourage your hearts and strengthen you in every good deed and word ... But the Lord is faithful, and he will strengthen and protect you from the evil one. We have confidence in the Lord that you are doing and will continue to do the things we command. May the Lord direct your hearts into God's love and Christ's perseverance.*

Dear Lord,

Thank you that your encouragement is eternal. Most days Yours is the only encouragement I receive. My hope is low, my heart is aching; yet I need only pull out my faithful Bible, and Your Living Word speaks strength into me, directing my heart back to the good hope, renewing my resolve to persevere through Jesus Christ. The Scriptures remind me of Your surpassing peace, Your protection from the evil one, Your constant presence, and most important of all, Your blessed assurance of salvation through Christ. I will stand firm in Your spiritual teachings, practicing them in my words and deeds.

# September

# 7

## 1 TIMOTHY 1;15–19

Dear Lord,

When You were on earth, thank you for choosing the people you did to spread the gospel. They were not the best of the best, the top 5% of High Achievers, the highly revered social elite. No, You picked ordinary fishermen like Simon, and awful people like Paul. Paul was one of the worst sinners of that time—he persecuted and killed Christians before his conversion. After his conversion he uttered the profound truth: Christ came to save sinners. The mercy shown to Paul is proof of Your unlimited love, that You want all Your creation to believe You are the One and Only God; that You sent Your only Son to die for our sins and rise again for our eternal salvation; it is left for us to only believe. I pray You help me fight the good fight to live for You in this world, holding on so my faith will not be shipwrecked by man nor minions of evil.

*Here is a trustworthy saying that deserves full acceptance: Christ Jesus came into the world to save sinners—of whom I am the worst. But for that very reason I was shown mercy so that in me, the worst of sinners, Christ Jesus might display his unlimited patience as an example for those who would believe on him and receive eternal life. Now to the King eternal, immortal, invisible, the only God, be honor and glory for ever and ever. Amen. Timothy, my son, I give you this instruction in keeping with the prophecies once made about you, so that by following them you may fight the good fight, holding on to faith and a good conscience. Some have rejected these and so have shipwrecked their faith.*

# September

# 8

### 1 TIMOTHY 2:1–6

*I urge, then, first of all, that requests, prayers, intercessions and thanksgiving be made for everyone—for kings and all those in authority, that we may live peaceful and quiet lives in all godliness and holiness. This is good, and pleases God our Savior, who wants all men to be saved and to come to a knowledge of the truth. For there is one God and one mediator between God and men, the man Christ Jesus, who gave himself as a ransom for all men—the testimony given in its proper time.*

Dear Lord,

I get so focused on immediate issues in my small sphere of the world, I hardly notice local, state, national or world concerns on a regular basis. Yet the outcome of those concerns may quickly affect my busy little life. I pray You watch over and guide those in authority, whether or not they have faith in You. You are sovereign, and will use whoever or whatever You want for Your purpose. In some small way, let my life lived for You be a positive, stabilizing force in this world, as multitudes of other believers do the same in their sphere of influence. May we continue to declare the Truth through our prayers, intercession for others, and thanksgiving for the ransom paid for our souls through Christ Jesus. May my professions of faith be sincere and given at the proper time so it will be received by the hearts You have prepared to hear.

# September

## 9

Dear Lord,

I do not want worldly riches, rather help me be content with the basics for living. Please provide me and my family with shelter, food, clothing, an education and transportation to be about Your business. Help me understand Your definition of what basics for living are, as mine may differ from yours. Please keep me from foolish and harmful desires which money may inspire. God forbid I ever wander from the faith; though I have wandered from Your Will at times, and as a result have been pierced with many griefs. May I always be thankful for Your provision, and use it wisely to give back to You.

### I TIMOTHY 6:6–10

*But godliness with contentment is great gain. For we brought nothing into the world, and we can take nothing out of it. But if we have food and clothing, we will be content with that. People who want to get rich fall into temptation and a trap and into many foolish and harmful desires that plunge men into ruin and destruction. For the love of money is a root of all kinds of evil. Some people, eager for money, have wandered from the faith and pierced themselves with many griefs.*

# September

# 10

## II TIMOTHY 1:7–11

*For God did not give us a spirit of timidity, but a spirit of power, of love and of self-discipline. So do not be ashamed to testify about our Lord, or ashamed of me his prisoner. But join with me in suffering for the gospel, by the power of God, who has saved us and called us to a holy life—not because of anything we have done but because of his own purpose and grace. This grace was given us in Christ Jesus before the beginning of time, but it has now been revealed through the appearing of our Savior, Christ Jesus, who has destroyed death and has brought life and immortality to light through the gospel. And of this gospel I was appointed a herald and an apostle and a teacher.*

Dear Lord,

It is my nature to be timid and shy. I have had to use self-discipline to force myself to be more outgoing. Despite my lack of self-confidence, empower me to visibly live a holy life. May others see my example, no, let them see through me to Your Example that lives in me through faith in Jesus Christ. Help others understand the Gospel, the Good News Jesus came to save mankind, destroy death, and replace it with eternal life; it is our choice to accept Your grace, or spend eternity without God. From my heart, know that I take seriously Your appointment of every believer to publicly acknowledge Your purpose is active in our lives. I am not ashamed of the Gospel of Jesus Christ.

# September

# 11

Dear Lord,

I must learn to rest from the busy-ness of life so I may be quiet enough for You to teach me how to enter into Your rest. Help me get there, because I know it will protect me from falling away from fellowship with You. I need to spend more time in Your Word to keep it living in me; it will adjust my heart's thoughts and attitudes. My soul is laid bare before You; I know I will have to give an account for all things I leave unresolved, unforgiven between You and me. I pray You keep me obedient and renewed through resting on Your promises.

## HEBREWS 4:9–13

*There remains, then, a Sabbath-rest for the people of God; for anyone who enters God's rest also rests from his own work, just as God did from his. Let us, therefore, make every effort to enter that rest, so that no one will fall by following their example of disobedience. For the word of God is living and active. Sharper than any double-edged sword, it penetrates even to dividing soul and spirit, joints and marrow; it judges the thoughts and attitudes of the heart. Nothing in all creation is hidden from God's sight. Everything is uncovered and laid bare before the eyes of him to whom we must give account.*

# September

# 12

### HEBREWS 4:14–16

*Therefore, since we have a great high priest who has gone through the heavens, Jesus the Son of God, let us hold firmly to the faith we profess. For we do not have a high priest who is unable to sympathize with our weaknesses, but we have one who has been tempted in every way, just as we are—yet was without sin. Let us then approach the throne of grace with confidence, so that we may receive mercy and find grace to help us in our time of need.*

Dear Lord,

For me, it is easier to speak to God the Son than God the Father. God the Father, in the Old Testament, ordered some dreadful things, because He is the righteous, holy God. But then He sent His Son to relate to humanity, to show us He understood our weaknesses, the temptations, the dreadful things mankind does, which is why God's judgment must come; and why the Son had to come, so we may approach the throne of grace for mercy rather than judgment. Thank you God the Father, God the Son, and God the Holy Spirit, for supplying in our time of need.

# September

# 13

Dear Lord,

Thank you for the reminder You will not forget. It isn't that I need acknowledgement for the things I do. But when I feel unnoticed, unappreciated and/or unloved most of the time, despite how much effort I put into my loved ones lives, or the lives of those I touch in my daily routine, it does get discouraging when no one is encouraging me back. I feel I am always pouring out, with nothing being poured back in. But You are continually pouring Your Spirit into me; You will not forget the diligence You have instilled in me. Your Promises are my hope; You notice, appreciate, love me—and that is the most important truth. Thank you for reminding me.

## HEBREWS 6:10–12

*God is not unjust; he will not forget your work and the love you have shown him as you have helped his people and continue to help them. We want each of you to show this same diligence to the very end, in order to make your hope sure. We do not want you to become lazy, but to imitate those who through faith and patience inherit what has been promised.*

# September

# 14

## HEBREWS 7:21–27

*… but he became a priest with an oath when God said to him: "The Lord has sworn and will not change his mind: 'You are a priest forever.'" Because of this oath, Jesus has become the guarantee of a better covenant. Now there have been many of those priests, since death prevented them from continuing in office; but because Jesus lives forever, he has a permanent priesthood. Therefore, he is able to save completely those who come to God through him, because he always lives to intercede for them. Such a high priest meets our need—one who is holy, blameless, pure, set apart from sinners, exalted above the heavens. Unlike the other high priests, he does not need to offer sacrifices day after day, first for his own sins, and then for the sins of the people. He sacrificed for their sins once for all when he offered himself.*

Dear Lord,

I understand now—no more priests are needed in the inner sanctuary of the temple because Jesus is the eternal priest. Though I have understood we have direct access to God, this scripture makes the significance of the temple veil being torn at the time of His temporary death even clearer! He saves completely because as the permanent priest He always lives to intercede, and His sacrifice was once and for all—the most perfect sacrifice. No more sacrifices at the temple need be made; I am truly humbled by this spiritual truth— thankful that all who believe may share in it.

Dear Lord,

Thank you that the time is here; the time when You have written Your laws upon the hearts of men. When Christ ascended to heaven, He left the Holy Spirit here with us so we may know You ourselves through prayer and Bible Study. The old ways of the prophets, animal and food sacrifices, harsh punishments, restrictions about food and drink, are gone. Now it is required that each one of us individually make the decision to enter in to the new covenant based on the sacrifice and resurrection of Jesus Christ. Through Christ the Law of Moses' time is made whole; rather than simply obeying rules out of fear, I embrace the Holy Scriptures as wise, lifesaving instruction from my heavenly Father, written with grace and mercy for my good and Your glory.

# September

# 15

## HEBREWS 8:8–13
### [QUOTING JEREMIAH 31:31–34]

*But God found fault with the people and said: "The time is coming, declares the Lord, when I will make a new covenant with the house of Israel and with the house of Judah. It will not be like the covenant I made with their forefathers when I took them by the hand to lead them out of Egypt, because they did not remain faithful to my covenant, and I turned away from them, declares the Lord. This is the covenant I will make with the house of Israel after that time, declares the Lord. I will put my laws in their minds and write them on their hearts. I will be their God, and they will be my people. No longer will a man teach his neighbor, or or a man his brother, saying 'Know the Lord,' because they will all know me, from the least of them to the greatest. For I will forgive their wickedness and will remember their sins no more." By calling this covenant "new," he has made the first one obsolete; and what is obsolete and aging will soon disappear.*

# September

# 16

## HEBREWS 10:22–25

*... let us draw near to God with a sincere heart in full assurance of faith, having our hearts sprinkled to cleanse us from a guilty conscience and having our bodies washed with pure water. Let us hold unswervingly to the hope we profess, for he who promised is faithful. And let us consider how we may spur one another on toward love and good deeds. Let us not give up meeting together, as some are in the habit of doing, but let us encourage one another—and all the more as you see the Day approaching.*

Dear Lord,

Your Word says I may be cleansed from a guilty conscience. I draw near to You, I ask, beg forgiveness for sin with a sincerely broken heart; yet I do not forgive myself. Thank you for the reminder I may have full assurance of faith; You forgave, I must do no less. I must hold unswervingly to my faith in You, because You are faithful. Help me be an encouragement to others, hoping they in turn will see it is You working through me. And help me when life gets too hectic or too painful to still make time to gather with Your people for worship, instruction, and to do Your work.

# September

# 17

Dear Lord,

Stand your ground—a difficult task when suffering and disappointment greet me at many turns. However I can persevere even when I lose my footing and/or fall. I will stand back up because my confidence is in Your promises—my heart's desire is to do Your Will. Help me keep the faith and not allow it to shrink in the face of adversity; for I know, whether my waters are calm or stormy, I am safe in Your arms.

## HEBREWS 10:32,35–39

*Remember those earlier days after you had received the light, when you stood your ground in a great contest in the face of suffering ... So do not throw away your confidence; it will be richly rewarded. You need to persevere so that when you have done the will of God, you will receive what he has promised. For in just a very little while, "He who is coming will come and will not delay. But my righteous one will live by faith. And if he shrinks back, I will not be pleased with him." But we are not of those who shrink back and are destroyed, but of those who believe and are saved.*

# September

# 18

## HEBREWS 11:1–3, 6

*Now faith is being sure of what we hope for and certain of what we do not see. This is what the ancients were commended for. By faith we understand that the universe was formed at God's command, so that what is seen was not made out of what was visible ... And without faith it is impossible to please God, because anyone who comes to him must believe that he exists and that he rewards those who earnestly seek him.*

Dear Lord,

This truth is so simple, yet so profound. This definition of faith: sure of what we hope for, certain of what we do not see. I am so grateful to You that I have faith in You, in the Holy Trinity, in Your Words contained in the Holy Bible. It is simple—I believe You exist, by faith I understand You formed the Universe by Your command. You spoke and it came into being. I have faith in Your Son, my intercessor before Your throne for my eternal salvation. In today's modern world, believing in the One True Deity is often considered narrow minded. Worse, men deify themselves, having their own version of spirituality that leads souls to being lost eternally. As for me, I earnestly seek You, growing in knowledge of You daily as You walk by my side.

# September

# 19

## JAMES 2:14–19

Dear Lord,

I have faith in You, the one true God. Knowing You, believing in You gives me the faith to act upon the promptings of the Holy Spirit, to be the ambassador of Christ you have called me to be. May my words, acts of compassion and understanding always be sincere, not an attempt to gain attention for myself. Rather may my deeds be the results of genuine faith and obedience to You.

*What good is it, my brothers, if a man claims to have faith but has no deeds? Can such faith save him? Suppose a brother or sister is without clothes and daily food. If one of you says to him, "Go, I wish you well; keep warm and well fed," but does nothing about his physical needs, what good is it? In the same way, faith by itself, if it is not accompanied by action, is dead. But someone will say, "You have faith; I have deeds." Show me your faith without deeds, and I will show you my faith by what I do. You believe that there is one God. Good! Even the demons believe that—and shudder.*

# September

# 20

## I PETER 3:8–12

*Finally, all of you, live in harmony with one another; be sympathetic, love as brothers, be compassionate and humble. Do not repay evil with evil or insult with insult, but with blessing, because to this you were called so that you may inherit a blessing. For, "Whoever would love life and see good days must keep his tongue from evil and his lips from deceitful speech. He must turn from evil and do good; he must seek peace and pursue it. For the eyes of the Lord are on the righteous and his ears are attentive to their prayer, but the face of the Lord is against those who do evil."*

Dear Lord,

Thank you for the compassion and blessing You give me every day. Because You have blessed me with Your presence, may I humbly show Your love and compassion to others. I want to be the good person You created me to be. Keep me from evil through the indwelling of Your Holy Spirit. I pray my eyes and ears are always attentive to Your still small voice so I may live in harmony with Your will, and impart Your peace onto my fellow man.

# September

# 21

Dear Lord,

I hunger and thirst after Your Bread of Life, the truth of Your Holy Word. I set myself apart from the world as Your servant. Imprint Your Spirit upon my soul; write Your Way into my heart; weave the Hope You give through salvation throughout the pattern of my life. I pray for Your guidance so I may mirror Christ's example by living a quiet and gentle life. Through humble prayer and repentance keep my conscience clear and my motives pure to honor Your Holy righteousness.

## I PETER 3:14–16

*But even if you should suffer for what is right, you are blessed. "Do not fear what they fear; do not be frightened." But in your hearts set apart Christ as Lord. Always be prepared to give an answer to everyone who asks you to give the reason for the hope that you have. But do this with gentleness and respect, keeping a clear conscience, so that those who speak maliciously against your good behavior in Christ may be ashamed of slander.*

# September

# 22

## I PETER 3:17–22

*It is better, if it is God's will, to suffer for doing good than for doing evil. For Christ died for sins once for all, the righteous for the unrighteous, to bring you to God. He was put to death in the body but made alive by the Spirit, through whom also he went and preached to the spirits in prison who disobeyed long ago when God waited patiently in the days of Noah while the ark was being built. In it only a few people, eight in all, were saved through water, and this water symbolizes baptism that now saves you also—not the removal of dirt from the body but the pledge of a good conscience toward God. It saves you by the resurrection of Jesus Christ, who has gone into heaven and is at God's right hand—with angels, authorities and powers in submission to him.*

Dear Lord,

Sometimes your teachings are hard to understand—why would it be Your Will we suffer for doing good? Then Your Spirit reminds me—to suffer for sinfulness is judgment; to suffer for good gives me a sense of the price my Righteous Lord paid for my sins. He who was only good died for me. You wait patiently for the world to recognize You before it is too late. Pledging allegiance to You gives me a good conscience, one washed in the flood of Your love, eagerly awaiting that day of Your return.

# September

# 23

Dear Lord,

Thank you for Your divine promises: Salvation through Jesus Christ, Your presence through the Holy Spirit, Your Living Word through the Holy Bible. I pray daily for increased heart knowledge of Your nature and Your ways so that through them I may live my life to honor and praise Your goodness and Your grace. Keep my heart from corruption through the indwelling of Your Holy Spirit. My soul's desire is to love my Savior, my One True God, with all my heart, mind and soul for all of my days—even through Eternity.

## II PETER 1:3–4

*His divine power has given us everything we need for life and godliness through our knowledge of him who called us by his own glory and goodness. Through these he has given us his very great and precious promises, so that through them you may participate in the divine nature and escape the corruption in the world caused by evil desires.*

# September

# 24

## II PETER 1:5–8

*For this very reason, make every effort to add to your faith goodness; and to goodness, knowledge; and to knowledge, self-control; and to self-control, perseverance; and to perseverance, godliness; and to godliness, brotherly kindness; and to brotherly kindness, love. For if you possess these qualities in increasing measure, they will keep you from being ineffective and unproductive in your knowledge of our Lord Jesus Christ.*

Dear Lord,

I pray for a daily infusion of Your strength to make me effective and productive for Your Kingdom. May I continually grow in faith and knowledge of Your ways; mold me into Your image so I may show others Your goodness. Teach me self-control over my actions and reactions, give me the ability to persevere through the trials and temptations of life. I strive for Your Godly image to be forever stamped on my soul, empowering me to be kind and loving to all Your children.

# September

# 25

Dear Lord,

Thank you for the faith You have given me; forgive me for the times it is weak. However, my belief You are the one true God, Jesus Christ is my Savior, and the Holy Spirit is dwelling within me is unshakeable through Your mercy and grace. I am deeply grateful for the many assurances Your Truth gives me. Regardless if You come for believers tomorrow or in ten thousand tomorrows—I know the God of all creation, the Righteous One, will return to take us to heaven and send the non-believers into eternity without Your presence. I believe, no matter if others do not because the world is too much before them. I pray for their deliverance, as You have delivered me.

## II PETER 3:3–7

*First of all, you must understand that in the last days scoffers will come, scoffing and following their own evil desires. They will say, "Where is the 'coming' he promised? Ever since our fathers died, everything goes on as it has since the beginning of creation." But they deliberately forget that long ago by God's word the heavens existed and the earth was formed out of water and by water. By these waters also the world of that time was deluged and destroyed. By the same word the present heavens and earth are reserved for fire, being kept for the day of judgment and destruction of ungodly men.*

# September

# 26

## II PETER 3:8–12A

*But do not forget this one thing, dear friends: With the Lord a day is like a thousand years, and a thousand years are like a day. The Lord is not slow in keeping his promises, as some understand slowness. He is patient with you, not wanting anyone to perish, but everyone to come to repentance. But the day of the Lord will come like a thief. The heavens will disappear with a roar; the elements will be destroyed by fire, and the earth and everything in it will be laid bare. Since everything will be destroyed in this way, what kind of people ought you be? You ought to live holy and godly lives as you look forward to the day of God and speed its coming.*

Dear Lord,

It does seem like forever and a day when I am waiting for my dreams to come true. Thank you You explain in Your Word your days are not on my days' time-line; it helps to know that. Not only should I be living a godly life striving to follow Your plan for my life, more importantly I need to be watchful and ready for Your return so when heaven and earth are no more, I do not perish rather I will gratefully live on in Your eternal presence.

# September

# 27

Dear Lord,

Thank you for lighting my way, beckoning me closer and closer to Your Way. When darkness threatens to envelop me, remind me not to fear what lay in the shadows, rather to keep my eyes upon the Way, the Truth and the Light. When I fade towards the darkness of fear and/or sin, remind me my fellowship is with You; my heart's desire is to walk in Truth with You, my sins covered by the blood of my Savior Jesus Christ.

## I JOHN 1:5–7

*This is the message we have heard from him and declare to you: God is light; in him there is no darkness at all. If we claim to have fellowship with him yet walk in the darkness, we lie and do not live by the truth. But if we walk in the light, as he is in the light, we have fellowship with one another, and the blood of Jesus, his Son, purifies us from all sin.*

# September

# 28

## I JOHN 3:16–20A

*This is how we know what love is: Jesus Christ laid down his life for us. And we ought to lay down our lives for our brothers. If anyone has material possessions and sees his brother in need but has no pity on him, how can the love of God be in him? Dear children, let us not love with words or tongue but with actions and in truth. This then is how we know that we belong to the truth, and how we set our hearts at rest in his presence whenever our hearts condemn us.*

Dear Lord,

Thank you for Your sacrificial example of what love is—giving Your earthly life for my sin. I want to give my life in service to others for Your glory. Whenever I feel worthless to Your Kingdom remind me, as I obediently have compassion and generosity in word and deed to my fellow man, my life is of use to You. As I pray and praise You, I belong to Your Truth—giving me peace in my heart.

# September

# 29

## 1 JOHN 5:11–15

Dear Lord,

Thank you for the gift of eternal life through Your Son. I think I ask for things according to Your Will; but I don't always get what I ask for. Sometimes it feels like You do not hear me. Remind me my confidence is in Your eternal love—You know what is best for me, and the best timing for all things. Let my life be a testimony to others of this faith in You, knowing that if my prayers are not answered the way I planned, they are answered according to Your plan.

*And this is the testimony: God has given us eternal life, and this life is in his Son. He who has the Son has life; he who does not have the Son of God does not have life. I write these things to you who believe in the name of the Son of God so that you may know that you have eternal life. This is the confidence we have in approaching God: that if we ask anything according to his will, he hears us. And if we know that he hears us—whatever we ask—we know that we have what we asked of him.*

# September

# 30

## REVELATIONS
### 3:8, 10–12A

*I know your deeds. See, I have placed before you an open door that no one can shut. I know that you have little strength, yet you have kept my word and have not denied my name ... Since you have kept my command to endure patiently, I will also keep you from the hour of trial that is going to come upon the whole world to test those who live on the earth. I am coming soon. Hold on to what you have, so that no one will take your crown. Him who overcomes I will make a pillar on the temple of my God.*

Dear Lord,

Though I have little strength, it is enough to hold on to Your Word. I acknowledge my faith in You in all my ways; You know my deeds. You know the trials I must overcome. As I endure faithfully with Your strength, you lead me along the path You have set before me, helping me avoid the pitfalls of this world, pulling me out of danger when I go astray, bestowing blessings upon me no one can take away. I will hold tightly to Your Hand until my journey ends at Your feet, then humbly lay my crown of life before Your Throne in eternal worship.

289

# Bow Before Him

# October

## 1

**PSALM
4:3–4**

*Know that the Lord has set apart the godly for himself; the Lord will hear when I call to him. In your anger do not sin; when you are on your beds, search your hearts and be silent.*

Dear Lord,

It is human nature to become angry, many times justifiably so. Please help me not use the fact I was truly wronged as justification for a hateful response—teach me to search my heart for Your Spirit's response, and remain silent enough to hear how I may defend myself without inappropriate retaliation in sinful anger. May I seek forgiveness when I have angered others by my poor behavior, knowing I have been set apart to serve You in a godly manner.

# October

# 2

## PSALM
26:2–3, 8, 12

*Test me, O Lord, and try me, examine my heart and my mind; for your love is ever before me, and I walk continually in your truth ... I love the house where you live, O Lord, the place where your glory dwells ... My feet stand on level ground; in the great assembly I will praise the Lord.*

Dear Lord,

I walk continually in Your truth—though I may struggle through the test and trials. Please examine my heart and mind, and show me where I need improvement, where I need change. Thank you for houses of worship, where I can assemble with other believers to praise You. I also praise Your loving presence in my life day by day, minute by minute, as You guide my feet towards You as if on level ground, though the way through this world is truly rough and rocky.

# October

# 3

**PSALM
30: 4–7**

Dear Lord,

I pray You do not get angry with me as I struggle to follow You faithfully. When I weep for forgiveness, I pray Your favor over my life is renewed as it was given the first day I accepted the sacrifice of Your Son, Jesus Christ. He is my strong mountain, He is my security, He is the reason I cannot be shaken, despite my imperfections that cause me dismay. I praise His Holy Name, and I sincerely want to serve God the Father, God the Son, and God the Holy Spirit through all the days of my life.

*Sing to the Lord, you saints of his; praise his holy name. For his anger lasts only a moment, but his favor lasts a lifetime; weeping may remain for a night, but rejoicing comes in the morning. When I felt secure, I said, "I will never be shaken." O Lord, when you favored me, you made my mountain stand firm; but when you hid your face, I was dismayed.*

# October

PSALM 34:1–6

*I will extol the Lord at all times; his praise will always be on my lips. My soul will boast in the Lord; let the afflicted hear and rejoice. Glorify the Lord with me; let us exalt his name together. I sought the Lord, and he answered me; he delivered me from all my fears. Those who look to him are radiant; their faces are never covered with shame. This poor man called, and the Lord heard him; he saved him out of all his troubles.*

Dear Lord,

At all times, in all circumstances, I give You the highest praise. In my soul I boast that I know the One True God as my Lord and Savior. As I struggle through trials, tribulations, temptations, remind me others who are afflicted are watching me; I must be an example who encourages them to glorify You, seeking You for deliverance from all their fears, no matter what they may be. And having been cleansed from the affliction of sin, I may lift my chin without shame, knowing I am keeping my covenant with you, my promise to love you with all my heart, soul and mind.

# October

# 5

Dear Lord,

When my cause feels hopeless, when my way is lonely and my heart's desires seem forever beyond my grasp, help me trust in You. Help me trust and <u>know</u> that You are working for my good and, as I follow Your way, I will do good for You with or without seeing my heart's desires come true. Living in Your land, I enjoy safe pasture in Your peaceful presence. My life is in Your hands.

## PSALM 37:3–6

*Trust in the Lord and do good; dwell in the land and enjoy safe pasture. Delight yourself in the Lord and he will give you the desires of your heart. Commit your way to the Lord; trust in him and he will do this: He will make your righteousness shine like the dawn, the justice of your cause like the noonday sun.*

# October

# 6

### PSALM
### 37:23–24, 27–28

*If the Lord delights in a man's way, he makes his steps firm; though he stumble, he will not fall, for the Lord upholds him with his hand … Turn from evil and do good; then you will dwell in the land forever. For the Lord loves the just and will not forsake his faithful ones.*

Dear Lord,

Please guide my steps firmly toward You, so that You will delight in the way I take. Thank You that when I stumble through my problems, You catch me as I fall and set me aright again. I love You with all my heart, soul, and mind; thank You for not forsaking me, despite my shortcomings, rather You see my sincere efforts to serve you faithfully. I pray You keep me from sin, leading me to be a blessing to others for Your glory.

# October

## PSALM 40:5–8

Dear Lord,

You have done wonderful things in my life—thank you for reminding me when I feel life is too much to bear. You do not require sacrifice and offerings; rather You want Your Word to pierce my soul—and it has. Here I am before you, humbled by Your love and mercy. I desire above all to do Your will; Your law, which was made complete through Jesus Christ, I will keep written upon my heart so it will guide my thoughts and actions, honoring You in all that I do.

*Many, O Lord my God, are the wonders you have done. The things you planned for us no one can recount to you; were I to speak and tell of them, they would be too many to declare. Sacrifice and offering you did not desire, but my ears you have pierced; burnt offerings and sin offerings you did not require. Then I said, "Here I am, I have come—it is written about me in the scroll. I desire to do your will, O my God; your law is within my heart."*

# October

## 8

### PSALM 56:12–13

*I am under vows to you, O God; I will present my thank offerings to you. For you have delivered me from death and my feet from stumbling, that I may walk before God in the light of life.*

Dear Lord,

I vow to follow You all the days of my life. You sacrificed your earthly life to deliver me from eternal death, and I humbly offer my everlasting gratitude. As I walk through this life, You lift me back up when I stumble, strengthen me when I am weary, continually heal me as I am among the walking wounded; You encourage and lighten my soul with your Holy Word. I give thank offerings to You for all the blessings and the challenges that mold me more and more into Your image. I pray I continually grow in Your knowledge and wisdom, that I may walk with Your light shining through me to touch others for Your glory.

Dear Lord,

When I am in distress, I seek You diligently. Night time is the worst, I am so alone. As I pray earnestly, I pray the same questions as the Psalmist: will You reject me forever, will You never show Your favor to me again, will Your promises never be fulfilled in my life though they are in others, has Your anger at my failings left me without Your mercy and compassion? My soul is not comforted until I feel Your Holy Spirit, who gently reminds me of the past, of all the previous favors, promises, mercies and compassions You have bestowed upon me. As I meditate on my blessings, I humbly pray forgiveness for questioning Your omniscient presence in my life, then peaceful sleep claims me as I rest in thankfulness for my God and Savior.

# October

# 9

## PSALM 77:1–3, 7–12

*I cried out to God for help; I cried out to God to hear me. When I was in distress, I sought the Lord; at night I stretched out untiring hands and my soul refused to be comforted. I remembered you, O God, and I groaned; I mused, and my spirit grew faint … "Will the Lord reject forever? Will he never show his favor again? Has his unfailing love vanished forever? Has his promise failed for all time? Has God forgotten to be merciful? Has he in anger withheld his compassion?" Then I thought, "To this I will appeal: the years of the right hand of the Most High." I will remember the deeds of the Lord; yes, I will remember your miracles of long ago. I will meditate on all your works and consider all your mighty deeds.*

# October

# 10

## PSALM 112:4–8

*Even in darkness light dawns for the upright, for the gracious and compassionate and righteous man. Good will come to him who is generous and lends freely, who conducts his affairs with justice. Surely he will never be shaken; a righteous man will be remembered forever. He will have no fear of bad news; his heart is steadfast, trusting in the Lord. His heart is secure, he will have no fear; in the end he will look in triumph on his foes.*

Dear Lord,

Though my faith is secure in You, I struggle with fears. Thank you for always being the beacon of light in such times of darkness, assuring me as I strive to be the gracious and compassionate soul You desire me to be, that You will help me be just and upright, even in the face of bad news. May my conduct model how a child of God responds; with faith and trust that the outcome is already decided by You, knowing that in the end You provide justice and peace for me—regardless of the attack of the enemy, whether it be upon me physically, mentally, emotionally. I have no fear spiritually because Your light shines eternally within my soul.

# October

# 11

Dear Lord,

As I sincerely seek You with all my heart, I pray You open my eyes and ears to your timeless truths. May I keep Your Wisdom in the forefront of my heart and mind. Remind me to consider Your ways in everything I do and say. I pray I will not neglect time spent with you, so I ask for a daily deepening of my walk with You through meditating on Your Word. I rejoice in Your goodness, letting it soothe my soul throughout my life as much as it is soothing me today.

## PSALM 119:10–18

*I seek you with all my heart; do not let me stray from your commands. I have hidden your word in my heart that I might not sin against you. Praise be to you, O Lord; teach me your decrees. With my lips I recount all the laws that come from your mouth. I rejoice in following your statutes as one rejoices in great riches. I meditate on your precepts and consider your ways. I delight in your decrees; I will not neglect your word. Do good to your servant, and I will live; I will obey your word. Open my eyes that I may see wonderful things in your law.*

# October

# 12

## PSALM 119:56–64

*This has been my practice: I obey your precepts. You are my portion, O Lord; I have promised to obey your words. I have sought your face with all my heart; be gracious to me according to your promise. I have considered my ways and have turned my steps to your statutes. I will hasten and not delay to obey your commands. Though the wicked bind me with ropes, I will not forget your law. At midnight I rise to give you thanks for your righteous laws. I am a friend to all who fear you, to all who follow your precepts. The earth is filled with your love, O Lord; teach me your decrees.*

Dear Lord,

Because I know of Your great mercy, it has been my practice to earnestly seek Your face for all my life. I pray for Your continued gracious companionship; it teaches me to consider my ways, and maintain my steps so they continually follow in Your ways. My soul compels me to obey your precepts and commands, as I know they lead to life eternal in Your peaceful presence. Even though wickedness attacks me or tries leading me astray, I pray Your precepts come to mind so I may live guided by Your righteous word.

# October

## 13

Dear Lord,

There is great knowledge in this world; combined with spiritual discernment I am able to understand much. Yet I am humbled there is so much more I do not know, great matters beyond my comprehension. Help me still my activities, quiet my soul, so I may listen and learn from You. Teach me to be the servant You have called me to be. Help me simply trust in You, as a young child trusts her mother, anticipating great and wonderful things throughout my life as my experiences make me grow in faith and hope.

### PSALM 131:1–3

*My heart is not proud, O Lord, my eyes are not haughty; I do not concern myself with great matters or things too wonderful for me. But I have stilled and quieted my soul; like a weaned child with its mother, like a weaned child is my soul within me. O Israel, put your hope in the Lord both now and forevermore.*

# October

# 14

## PSALM
## 139:17–18, 23–24

*How precious to me are your thoughts, O God! How vast is the sum of them! Were I to count them, they would outnumber the grains of sand. When I awake, I am still with you … Search me, O God, and know my heart; test me and know my anxious thoughts. See if there is any offensive way in me, and lead me in the way everlasting.*

Dear Lord,

Your Word is so precious to me because of the knowledge and wisdom it imparts. The Bible leads me as I seek Your thoughts towards me; as I pray for discernment about Your specific plan for me, Your Holy Spirit writes it upon my heart. I sincerely pray You search my heart; purge me of any offensive ways. Test me; help me pass the trials and tribulations on Your Strength and not my own. When I lean on my own strength and understanding, it often leads to anxious thoughts; bring me back to what is written in Your Word and imprinted upon my heart, and lead me in the way I must go.

# October

# 15

## PSALM
141:2–4, 8

Dear Lord,

I pray my behavior honors You, that my time of worship pleases You. When I am drawn towards disobeying Your Word, keep watch over my lips and my actions. Though the gate is open wide, keep me from entering in to wicked ways. Wayward souls may seem to prosper for a time; however, I know the end is death without Your saving grace. Guard my words to others as it is not mine to judge which way they will go, only to live with my eyes fixed upon You, living the quiet life of a sincere believer. In worship I lift my heart and hands toward my Sovereign Lord, for I know where my help comes from; I know You are my eternal refuge.

*May my prayer be set before you like incense; may the lifting up of my hands be like the evening sacrifice. Set a guard over my mouth, O Lord; keep watch over the door of my lips. Let not my heart be drawn to what is evil, to take part in wicked deeds with men who are evildoers; let me not eat of their delicacies … But my eyes are fixed on you, O Sovereign Lord; in you I take refuge—do not give me over to death.*

# October

# 16

## EXODUS 20:17
[10th Commandment]

*"You shall not covet your neighbor's house. You shall not covet your neighbor's wife, or his manservant or maidservant, his ox or donkey, or anything that belongs to your neighbor."*

## HEBREWS 13:5–6

*Keep your lives free from the love of money and be content with what you have, because God has said, "Never will I leave you; never will I forsake you." So we say with confidence, "The Lord is my helper; I will not be afraid. What can man do to me?"*

Dear Lord,

Is it covetous to want financial stability like others have? Is it improper to want a loving mate in a peaceful home like others have? It is not that I want those things in a selfish way, I do not want to have those blessings instead of them, I want those blessings along with them. I have needed, have hoped and prayed, for these blessings all my life. But I do not have those blessings. Thank you for reminding me, though I do not have the same blessings as others, I am richly blessed through Your love—You provide my daily needs financially, physically and emotionally. Teach me to be content with my lot in life, if for no other reason, than that I can be confident You will always be in my life.

# October

# 17

## DEUTERONOMY
4:39–40

*Acknowledge and take heart this day that the Lord is God in heaven above and on the earth below. There is no other. Keep his decrees and commands, which I am giving you today, so that it may go well with you and your children after you and that you may live long in the land the Lord your God gives you for all time.*

Dear Lord,

As a believer, the easy part is acknowledging You are Lord God of all the heavens—the hard part is constantly feeling Your Presence with me here on earth. I do my best to keep Your decrees and commands, teach them to my children; but it does not always go well with me. I may doubt You are near, that You are at work within my lonely broken heart. Lord, take my brokenness within Your protective, nail scarred hands; heal it and keep it safe from continual attacks of the ruler of this world. Gently remind me daily, whether the day goes well or no, that I am spiritually well because You are Lord God in heaven and earth, and eternally live within my heart.

# October

# 18

### DEUTERONOMY 5:32–33

*So be careful to do what the Lord your God has commanded you; do not turn aside to the right or to the left. Walk in all the ways that the Lord your God has commanded you, so that you may live and prosper and prolong your days in the land that you will possess.*

Dear Lord,

Sometimes no matter how careful I am, I lose my way. I do not mean to—circumstances or obstacles obscure the path. At those times, remind me to close my eyes, not turn to the right or to the left, but to listen for Your voice, then continue to walk in Your way.

# October

# 19

Dear Lord,

Teach me to live by Your Word. Cause me to hunger for Your promises, the ones specifically for me. Test me, know my heart, lead me to the 'land' You want me to possess though all I see is desert. Show me Your promises did not expire with ancient times, for Your Holy Word is as true today as it was at the beginning of time. As I wander through my own private wilderness, feed me with spiritual manna, filling me with Your presence until I reach eternal contentment.

## DEUTERONOMY 8:1–3

*Be careful to follow every command I am giving you today, so that you may live and increase and may enter and possess the land the Lord promised on oath to your forefathers. Remember how the Lord God led you all the way in the desert these forty years, to humble you and to test you in order to know what was in your heart, whether or not you would keep his commands. He humbled you, causing you to hunger and then feeding you with manna, which neither you nor your fathers had known, to teach you that man does not live on bread alone but on every word that comes from the mouth of the Lord.*

# October

# 20

## DEUTERONOMY 10:12–13

*And now, O Israel, what does the Lord your God ask of you but to fear the Lord your God, to walk in all his ways, to love him, to serve the Lord your God with all your heart and with all your soul, and to observe the Lord's commands and decrees that I am giving you today for your own good.*

Dear Lord,

Fearing eternity without You, I embrace with faith that You exist. When I am going through difficult choices, help me remember that what You ask of me is for my own good. Therefore, with courage I face my earthly challenges. With a servant's heart and thankful soul, enable me to obey the Truth of Your Word.

# October
# 21

Dear Lord,

Modern society has plenty of false gods, even if they are not represented by physical idols. Materialism, excessive egos, Hollywood fame, ruthless success, selfish and thoughtless ambitions, all can usurp Your rightful throne in people's hearts. May I always be able to say, as Joshua did centuries ago, 'But as for me and my household, we will serve the Lord.' It is my deepest desire to be ever faithful to You—lead me in Your ways.

## JOSHUA 24:14–15

*"Now fear the Lord and serve him with all faithfulness. Throw away the gods your forefathers worshiped beyond the River and in Egypt, and serve the Lord. But if serving the Lord seems undesirable to you, then choose for yourselves this day whom you will serve, whether the gods your forefathers served beyond the River, or the gods of the Amorites, in whose land you are living. But as for me and my household, we will serve the Lord."*

# October

# 22

## II SAMUEL 22:24–30

*I have been blameless before him and have kept myself from sin. The Lord has rewarded me according to my righteousness, according to my cleanness in his sight. To the faithful you show yourself faithful, to the blameless you show yourself blameless, to the pure you show yourself pure, but to the crooked you show yourself shrewd. You save the humble, but your eyes are on the haughty to bring them low. You are my lamp, O Lord; the Lord turns my darkness into light. With your help I can advance against a troop; with my God I can scale a wall.*

Dear Lord,

Oh how I need Your lamp to guide me! Otherwise the darkness envelopes me, the walls enclose about me and I am forever lost. With Your light to guide me, I will advance in faithfulness, blamelessness, purity and humility. I pray You always keep my path from going crooked, rather may it always lead straight to You. With Your light, I can keep myself from the sin that abounds. But should I stray, save me from disaster through Your grace and mercy. With You, I once again enter the battle prepared to defeat the enemy of my soul.

# October

# 23

Dear Lord,

Why would You leave the peaceful haven of the spiritual realm to be mocked and murdered by ungrateful mortals? After Your resurrection, why did You still remain in spiritual form, dwelling among us within the hearts of believers? My soul is at Your mercy; I offer my heart as a temple for my Holy God and my hands to do Your work. You have my deepest gratitude for the blessings You bestow upon me: my family, my means of financial support, my home, my daily needs; but most of all, for Your comforting, constant presence that envelopes my soul.

## II CHRONICLES 6:18–19

*But will God really dwell on earth with men? The heavens, even the highest heavens, cannot contain you. How much less this temple I have built! Yet give attention to your servant's prayer and his plea for mercy, O Lord my God. Hear the cry and the prayer that your servant is praying in your presence.*

# October

# 24

## II CHRONICLES 7:13–16

*"When I shut up the heavens so that there is no rain, or command locusts to devour the land or send a plague among my people, if my people, who are called by my name, will humble themselves and pray and seek my face and turn from their wicked ways, then I will hear from heaven, and I will forgive their sin and will heal their land. Now my eyes will be open and my ears attentive to the prayers offered in this place. I have chosen and consecrated this temple so that my Name may be there forever. My eyes and my heart will always be there."*

Dear Lord,

When You allow all manner of plagues, of struggles to enter my life, humbly I seek Your face for deliverance. Cleanse me of my sins, heal my brokenness, and consecrate the center of my soul as Your spiritual temple. Guide me through life's trials and triumphs until I am safely in Your heavenly presence for all time.

# October

# 25

## II CHRONICLES 30:8–9

Dear Lord,

Every time I fail You, I sincerely, humbly return to You, deeply grateful for Your grace and compassion. Forgive my poor example before others; defeat my rebel thoughts and actions that deserve Your righteous judgement. Create in me a servant's heart; may my submission to Your Will show others they too can be free from the captivity of sin through Your mercy. Consecrate my heart and soul as a sanctuary of worship for You, my Lord and Savior.

*"Do not be stiff-necked, as your fathers were; submit to the Lord. Come to the sanctuary, which he has consecrated forever. Serve the Lord your God, so that his fierce anger will turn away from you. If you return to the Lord, then your brothers and your children will be shown compassion by their captors and will come back to this land, for the Lord your God is gracious and compassionate. He will not turn his face from you if you return to him."*

# October

# 26

## JOB 22:21–22, 23:10–12

*[Eliphaz:] Submit to God and be at peace with him; in this way prosperity will come to you. Accept instruction from his mouth and lay up his words in your heart.*

*[Job:] But he knows the way I take; when he has tested me, I will come forth as gold. My feet have closely followed his steps; I have kept to his way without turning aside. I have not departed from the commands of his lips; I have treasured the words of his mouth more than my daily bread.*

Dear Lord,

You know the way I take, You know how closely I follow You, treasure Your Word in my heart, and the fellowship with Your Holy Spirit. I faithfully practice Your commands, yet, prosperity eludes me; still, I am at peace with Your daily provision. Your Spirit lets me know lack of success in worldly ways is not a reflection of lack in my spiritual ways. Rather, I have been chosen to be tested by trials; I pray that I too, like Job, will come forth as pure gold through Your cleansing fire.

# October

# 27

Dear Lord,

I am guilty of asking Almighty God why, why me? Why don't You answer me about this or that, why don't You fix this or that? Help me perceive the different ways You speak to me, and may I listen attentively to what You have to say. I pray for discernment when I am to wait before You because it is not yet time for Your answer, or to be prepared to follow Your lead in another direction than I would have chosen.

## JOB 33:12–14

*But I tell you, in this you are not right, for God is greater than man. Why do you complain to him that he answers none of man's words? For God does speak—now one way, now another— though man may not perceive it.*

# October

# 28

## JOB 40:1–5

*The Lord said to Job: "Will the one who contends with the Almighty correct him? Let him who accuses God answer him!" Then Job answered the Lord: "I am unworthy—how can I reply to you? I put my hand over my mouth. I spoke once, but I have no answer—twice, but I will say no more."*

Dear Lord,

There are times I am sure my questioning 'why' is contentious to You—there are pieces of the puzzle I do not have, there are spiritual battles I do not see, there are reasons beyond my comprehension for life to be the way it is. How can I accuse the Creator of the Universe of not doing things right or at the right time? I am humbled by Your Majesty. Through faith I have confidence You are in control of my life, and thankful that I am not.

# October

# 29

**PROVERBS 7:1–3**

*My son, keep my words and store up my commands within you. Keep my commands and you will live; guard my teachings as the apple of your eye. Bind them on your fingers; write them on the tablet of your heart.*

Dear Lord,

Thank you for imprinting Your Spirit upon my soul. I want to keep Your commands; write them indelibly upon the tablet of my heart. I pray You give me the ability to store Your words in my mind for a ready answer. Guard my heart and mind so that Your teachings will be with me all the days of my life.

# October

# 30

## PROVERBS
### 13:13–16

*He who scorns instruction will pay for it, but he who respects a command is rewarded. The teaching of the wise is a fountain of life, turning a man from the snares of death. Good understanding wins favor, but the way of the unfaithful is hard. Every prudent man acts out of knowledge, but a fool exposes his folly.*

Dear Lord,

Protect me from the folly of a fool. Encourage me to seek Your instruction in all things so I do not suffer needless pain from avoidable consequences if only I had listened. At the same time, help me discern the times when circumstances are just because I live in this imperfect world rather than the consequences of my failure to hear Your commands. Keep me teachable through Your Holy Spirit and Your Word, my actions driven by knowledge of You. I know my reward is living an eternity in Your presence.

# October

# 31

### PROVERBS
16:21–24

Dear Lord,

My sincere prayer is for You to give me pleasant, healing words for others. I pray for discernment to know when to speak, when to hold my tongue, waiting for Your instruction. Let me be a sweet blessing to a hurting soul, even though I may never know it, You see into the depths of their solitude, just as You do into mine. Oh how I have longed for wisdom in my darkest times of solitude, and You provide it! When I am crushed to the bone, Your Word brings sweet healing to them, and with Your guidance I continue the journey of life.

*The wise in heart are called discerning, and pleasant words promote instruction. Understanding is a fountain of life to those who have it, but folly brings punishment to fools. A wise man's heart guides his mouth, and his lips promote instruction. Pleasant words are a honeycomb, sweet to the soul and healing to the bones.*

# November

## 1

### PROVERBS
25:21–22, 26:20

*If your enemy is hungry, give him food to eat; if he is thirsty, give him water to drink. In doing this, you will heap burning coals on his head, and the Lord will reward you ... without wood a fire goes out; without gossip a quarrel dies down.*

Dear Lord,

I may not have enemies trying to literally take my life as the psalmist did, but I do have adversaries in certain situations whom cause me struggles. Help me maintain an appropriate attitude when faced with opposition; keep me calm, fair and respectful as each situation requires. Let my verbal contributions move toward resolution rather than prolong the fire of conflict.

# November

# 2

### ECCLESIASTES
12:13–14

*Now all has been heard; here is the conclusion of the matter: Fear God and keep his commandments, for this is the whole duty of man. For God will bring every deed into judgment, including every hidden thing, whether it is good or evil.*

Dear Lord,

I believe that after everything has been said, heard, or done, what ultimately matters is that I have done my duty for You. Out of fear in the sense that I know Your Word is true—if I follow You I go to heaven; if I do not I go to hell. However, in the true sense I serve my duty to You out of love because You first loved me, even though You know my hidden deeds, hidden fears, hidden hopes. From my beginning to my end, You are my Hope.

# November

# 3

### ISAIAH 5:11–12

*Woe to those who rise early in the morning to run after their drinks, who stay up late at night till they are inflamed with wine. They have harps and lyres at their banquets, tambourines and flutes and wine, but they have no regard for the deeds of the Lord, no respect for the work of his hands.*

Dear Lord,

I have the utmost respect for the work of Your mighty hands, and reverent regard for Your marvelous deeds. I do not understand how those who do not respect and revere You are able to prosper, as well as enjoy their indulgent lifestyle while it seems the woeful trials are plentiful for Your believers. Yet I will remain faithful because as time passes, I see You continually move in my life in ways they cannot know, until they also turn their lives over to You.

# November

Dear Lord,

Thank you for Your Holy Spirit, the discernment He brings to my heart and soul. Thank you that through Jesus Christ's example on earth we see how Your Spirit rests upon our lives as we follow You, seeking Your wisdom, understanding, counsel, power and knowledge. You are my righteousness and it is my desire to be faithful to You, my Savior and Lord.

## ISAIAH 11:2–5

*The Spirit of the Lord will rest on him—the Spirit of wisdom and of understanding, the Spirit of counsel and of power, the Spirit of knowledge and of the fear of the Lord—and he will delight in the fear of the Lord. He will not judge by what he sees with his eyes, or decide by what he hears with his ears; but with righteousness he will judge the needy, with justice he will give decisions for the poor of the earth. He will strike the earth with the rod of his mouth; with the breath of his lips he will slay the wicked. Righteousness will be his belt and faithfulness the sash around his waist.*

# November

# 5

## ISAIAH 32:17–18

*The fruit of righteousness will be peace; the effect of righteousness will be quietness and confidence forever. My people will live in peaceful dwelling places, in secure homes, in undisturbed places of rest.*

Dear Lord,

Peace, quietness, confidence—how I long for these blessings in my life! Despite worldly temptations, lead me in a righteous life as one of Your people. May I abide secure with Your presence, though things around me may disturb my soul.

# November

# 6

Dear Lord,

Thank you You laid this scripture on my heart so long ago, giving me hope when I was hopeless. But how can I forget the former things when the hurt can be so intense it is hard to breathe? Please show me the way through this wasteland to Your peace. I have been lost in this wilderness for so long. Open my eyes to new blessings, the daily blessings, You have for me as I follow You all the days of my life.

## ISAIAH 43:18–19

*Forget the former things; do not dwell on the past. See, I am doing a new thing! Now it springs up; do you not perceive it? I am making a way in the desert and streams in the wasteland.*

# November

# 7

ISAIAH 46:5, 8–10

*To whom will you compare me or count me equal? To whom will you liken me that we may be compared? … Remember this, fix it in mind, take it to heart, you rebels. Remember the former things, those of long ago; I am God, and there is no other; I am God, and there is none like me. I make known the end from the beginning, from ancient times, what is still to come. I say: My purpose will stand, and I will do all that I please.*

Dear Lord,

I believe You are God; it is fixed in my soul there is no other. There is no comparison when I look elsewhere; only You clothed Yourself in flesh in the form of Your Only Son thousands of years ago. You sent Him to die and rise again to save us, those whom You created in Your own image. Only You left Your divine Holy Spirit on earth to dwell within Your believers' hearts to carry out Your purpose. May Your purpose stand in my heart, mind and soul, regardless of the cares or false answers this world presents to me. You hold my past, present and future; I continually lay my life on the altar at Your feet for You to do as You please with this humble servant.

# November

# 8

Dear Lord,

I am standing at a crossroads. There are many ways to take—help me make the right decisions. I ask that You guide me with Your ancient wisdom, that You lead me down the good way, and even though it is not the easiest way, help me follow it. Assure me that after I have made the right decision, I will have peace in my soul, and rest in Your continued presence.

## JEREMIAH 6:16

*This is what the Lord says: "Stand at the crossroads and look; ask for the ancient paths, ask where the good way is, and walk in it, and you will find rest for your souls...."*

# November

# 9

## EZEKIEL 18:20–23

*The soul who sins is the one who will die. The son will not share the guilt of the father, nor will the father share the guilt of the son. The righteousness of the righteous man will be credited to him, and the wickedness of the wicked will be charged against him. But if a wicked man turns away from all the sins he has committed and keeps all my decrees and does what is just and right, he will surely live; he will not die. None of the offenses he has committed will be remembered against him. Because of the righteous things he has done, he will live. Do I take any pleasure in the death of the wicked? declares the Sovereign Lord. Rather, am I not pleased when they turn from their ways and live?*

Dear Lord,

Thank you we are responsible only for the consequences of our own decisions where spiritual matters are concerned. Though we may not understand why the wicked are able to harm innocents, we have Your assurance that if the victim followed you, their soul is safe even if the body was not. Your grace is given to all who turn from sin and seek Your righteousness. I pray for those who resist knowing You; if they continue without spiritual forgiveness of sin, it will lead to death. I pray, instead, they will turn to You, committing themselves under Your mercy and grace.

# November

# 10

Dear Lord,

Please never let me stray from faith in You. Please do not let me judge another's sinful behavior, as mine also offends Your sovereignty. May Your Holy Spirit turn me away from any unfaithfulness and continually renew my heart and spirit according to Your Will. Thank you that when Judgment Day arrives You will remember I have loved You with a sincere heart; I have repented and been cleansed by the blood of the Lamb, and His righteousness covers my soul for eternity.

## EZEKIEL 18:24, 27–28, 30–31

*But if a righteous man turns from his righteousness and commits sin and does the same detestable things the wicked man does, will he live? None of the righteous things he has done will be remembered. Because of the unfaithfulness he is guilty of and because of the sins he has committed, he will die ... But if a wicked man turns away from the wickedness he has committed and does what is just and right, he will save his life. Because he considers all the offenses he has committed and turns away from them, he will surely live; he will not die ... Therefore, O house of Israel, I will judge you, each one according to his ways, declares the Sovereign Lord. Repent! Turn away from all your offenses; then sin will not be your downfall. Rid yourselves of all the offenses you have committed, and get a new heart and a new spirit.*

# November

# 11

## ZEPHANIAH
### 2:1–3, 3:17

*Gather together, gather together, O shameful nation, before the appointed time arrives and that day sweeps on like chaff, before the fierce anger of the Lord comes upon you, before the day of the Lord's wrath comes upon you. Seek the Lord, all you humble of the land, you who do what he commands. Seek righteousness, seek humility; perhaps you will be sheltered on the day of the Lord's anger ... The Lord your God is with you, he is mighty to save. He will take great delight in you, he will quiet you with his love, he will rejoice over you with singing.*

Dear Lord,

I humbly come before you, knowing my sins and inadequacies, seeking the covering of Your righteousness before it can be found no more. Because of Your great mercy, thank you for sparing me Your full anger which sin deserves; thank you that, just like the worthless chaff is separated from the seeds of grain, the wind of Your Holy Spirit sweeps away the useless debris in my life, and plants the seeds of Your Word to nourish and grow in my heart and soul. Thank you for knowing that I do my best to follow Your commands, and when my best is not good enough because my strength fails, You remind me it is Your strength that brings out the best in me. Once I remember this, You quiet the turmoil inside me, and I rejoice in the presence of the Lord.

# November

# 12

### MATTHEW
### 5:44–45

*But I tell you: Love your enemies and pray for those who persecute you, that you may be sons of your Father in heaven. He causes his sun to rise on the evil and the good, and sends rain on the righteous and unrighteous.*

Dear Lord,

How can I pray for the person who has destroyed my marriage, harmed my children, or damaged my credibility within my profession? And got away with it? Why is the sun shining for him or her, and I'm drowning in the rain of my tears? Regardless why, I see that my bitterness only sours my life, not theirs. Help me forgive them as You have instructed, and pray for them so they will seek You and not hurt others in these ways again; as for me, I seek Your peace to rest within my soul.

# November

# 13

## MATTHEW 28:16–20

*Then the eleven disciples went to Galilee, to the mountain where Jesus had told them to go. When they saw him, they worshiped him; but some doubted. Then Jesus came to them and said, "All authority in heaven and on earth has been given to me. Therefore go and make disciples of all nations, baptizing them in the name of the Father and of the Son and of the Holy Spirit, and teaching them to obey everything I have commanded you. And surely I am with you always, to the very end of the age."*

Dear Lord,

I worship You for who You are, Father, Son, and Holy Spirit. I know You are at work in my life; may I obey and follow Your lead without doubts. However, when the struggle is long, and my spirit is weak, I regret I do doubt since I cannot see Your plan. In those times, may I hold on to Your Word which tells me You have all authority. As I live under Your authority, with faith I always eventually see Your plans for my life unfold. I pray that as I track with Your commands along the narrow way to eternity, others witness Your faithfulness and learn to follow You too.

Dear Lord,

How could these two disciples be so arrogant as to ask You to sit on either side of You as rulers in heaven?! How can they be so bold as to believe You would give them whatever they ask? Yet sometimes my prayers must sound like theirs, "Lord, I need you to do this, this and that, and could You make sure it is done by the time I wake up in the morning?" Forgive me for being so presumptuous; my assignment on earth is to follow your teachings. I need a servant's heart to do Your work. If I am in authority over others, may I humbly fulfill the responsibility entrusted to me. When I am tempted to be prideful in my own greatness, remind me that it is You who gave me abilities to share their fruits with others. Thank you for the blessings You have bestowed on this humble servant.

# November

# 14

## MARK 10:35–37, 41–45

*Then James and John, the sons of Zebedee, came to him. "Teacher," they said, "we want you to do for us whatever we ask." "What do you want me to do for you?" he asked. They replied, "Let one of us sit at your right and the other at your left in your glory." … When the ten heard about this, they became indignant with James and John. Jesus called them together and said, "You know that those who are regarded as rulers of the Gentiles lord it over them, and their high officials exercise authority over them. Not so with you. Instead, whoever wants to become great among you must be your servant, and whoever wants to be first must be slave of all. For even the Son of Man did not come to be served, but to serve, and to give his life as a ransom for many."*

# November

# 15

## LUKE 17:1–4

*Jesus said to His disciples: "Things that cause people to sin are bound to come, but woe to that person through whom they come. It would be better for him to be thrown into the sea with a millstone tied around his neck than for him to cause one of these little ones to sin. So watch yourselves. If your brother sins, rebuke him, and if he repents, forgive him. If he sins against you seven times in a day, and seven times comes back to you and says, 'I repent,' forgive him."*

Dear Lord,

Thank you for the forgiveness given to me through accepting Jesus Christ as my Lord and Savior. May I influence others to follow You; with tears I ask forgiveness if I have been the cause for another to stumble. Examine my life, teach me Your ways, show me the path away from sinful deeds. As You are merciful to me, compel me to be merciful and forgive those whose sin affects me—give me a way out that I may be an example of a life honoring You.

# November

# 16

Dear Lord,

Thank you that hard times and painful hurts are not necessarily my own fault. Rather the trials and tribulations allow You to work in my life, and as I trust You to see me through, may others see the miracles of deliverance whether they be physically or spiritually dramatic, or quietly consistent with a godly life. You are the light of my world; sometimes just a pin prick of light on the horizon of my darkness giving me hope, other times Your full glory shines on my face as I praise You for Your constant loving care.

## JOHN 9:1–5

*As he went along, he saw a man blind from birth. His disciples asked him, "Rabbi, who sinned, this man or his parents, that he was born blind?" "Neither this man nor his parents sinned," said Jesus, "but this happened so that the work of God might be displayed in his life. As long as it is day, we must do the work of him who sent me. Night is coming, when no one can work. While I am in the world, I am the light of the world."*

# November

# 17

## JOHN 15:9–14

*As the Father has loved me, so have I loved you. Now remain in my love. If you obey my commands, you will remain in my love, just as I have obeyed my Father's commands and remain in his love. I have told you this so that my joy may be in you and that your joy may be complete. My command is this: Love each other as I have loved you. Greater love has no one than this, that he lay down his life for his friends. You are my friends if you do what I command.*

Dear Lord,

Thank you for laying down Your life for me on the cross. I know there is no greater sacrifice. You became God in the flesh to save me, and rose from the cross to prepare heaven for all believers. Given Your example of sacrifice, I must do no less: I lay down my life in service to You. My desire is to be like You, show love for those in my circle of influence, whether closest relative or farthest acquaintance. I want to do what is good and right in Your eyes as a testament of my devotion to You. Your commands are not burdensome, for they make my spirit prosper, and Your love brings joy in all situations. Prosper by being rich in spirit, and joyful that my name is written in the Book of Life.

# November

# 18

### JOHN 21:17-22

*The third time he said to him, "Simon son of John, do you love me?" Peter was hurt because Jesus asked him the third time, "Do you love me?" He said, "Lord you know all things; you know that I love you." Jesus said, "Feed my sheep. I tell you the truth, when you were younger you dressed yourself and went where you wanted; but when you are old you will stretch out your hands, and someone else will dress you and lead you where you do not want to go." Jesus said this to indicate the kind of death by which Peter would glorify God. Then he said to him, "Follow me!" Peter turned and saw that the disciple whom Jesus loved was following them. (This was the one who had leaned back against Jesus at the supper and had said, "Lord, who is going to betray you?") When Peter saw him, he asked, "Lord what about him?" Jesus answered, "If I want him to remain alive until I return, what is that to you? You must follow me."*

Dear Lord,

Sometimes I feel like Simon Peter, I tell You I love You as I pray for guidance and deliverance, but all I hear is what I already know—feed Your sheep, be an example of Christ. I see others serving You, perhaps less zealously than I, yet they are getting answers to prayers while You are still silent to mine. How can this be? Help me in my struggle to understand, just as You helped Peter— that it doesn't matter how things work out for others, I must follow You through my life's journey, no matter the cost.

# November

# 19

## ROMANS 12:1–3

*Therefore, I urge you, brothers, in view of God's mercy, to offer your bodies as living sacrifices, holy and pleasing to God—this is your spiritual act of worship. Do not conform any longer to the pattern of this world, but be transformed by the renewing of your mind. Then you will be able to test and approve what God's will is—his good, pleasing and perfect will. For by the grace given me I say to every one of you: Do not think of yourself more highly than you ought, but rather think of yourself with sober judgment, in accordance with the measure of faith God has given you.*

Dear Lord,

The pattern of this world—as a society it has an ever growing selfishness within individuals that causes so much heartache and destruction. Knowingly or not, some are a god unto themselves, seeking whatever pleases them with callous disregard for the collateral damage their actions may cause. They put themselves first above all, ignoring Your Lordship. Help me not conform to the temptation of being self-absorbed; may I daily, moment by moment, be committed to renewing my mind with Your Truths. I offer my heart, soul and mind as a sacrifice of worship, by faith seeking Your will for my life.

# November

# 20

Dear Lord,

I am not one of the strong. There are times I am sure I have reached the limit of my endurance; I feel the world is too much for me and all hope is gone. Thank you for writing the Holy Bible—for Your Scriptures are full of human trauma and unfailing spiritual hope. Your Word is alive and speaks encouragement, peace and rest to my soul, assuring me that though I am weak, You are strong. May I help others through the power of the Holy Spirit, and be the blessing You have called me to be.

ROMANS 15:1–4,13

*We who are strong ought to bear with the failings of the weak and not to please ourselves. Each of us should please his neighbor for his good, to build him up. For even Christ did not please himself but, as it is written: "The insults of those who insult you have fallen on me." For everything that was written in the past was written to teach us, so that through endurance and the encouragement of the Scriptures we might have hope ... May the God of hope fill you with all joy and peace as you trust in him, so that you may overflow with hope by the power of the Holy Spirit.*

# November

# 21

## I CORINTHIANS 10:12–13

*So, if you think you are standing firm, be careful that you don't fall! No temptation has seized you except what is common to man. And God is faithful; he will not let you be tempted beyond what you can bear. But when you are tempted, he will also provide a way out so that you can stand up under it.*

Dear Lord,

When I was younger, it was so easy to quote this scripture and live by it. The way out of temptation was clear and fairly easy to follow. Now that I am older, life's battle wounds have made me weaker, yet they have also made me wiser. Some things are not as clear cut and easy as I used to think. I truly understand being 'seized' by temptation, and the way out may be obscured behind all-consuming pain and fear. I feel it is too much for me to bear. Then, because You are faithful, You remind me You are ever present. You stand me up, show me the way out, and clear that path for my escape.

# November

# 22

## I CORINTHIANS
10:23–24, 31–33, 11:1

*'Everything is permissible'—but not everything is beneficial. 'Everything is permissible'—but not everything is constructive. Nobody should seek his own good, but the good of others … . So whether you eat or drink or whatever you do, do it all for the glory of God. Do not cause anyone to stumble, whether Jews, Greeks or the church of God—even as I try to please everybody in every way. For I am not seeking my own good but the good of many, so that they may be saved. Follow my example, as I follow the example of Christ.*

Dear Lord,

You understand everything I do, you understand all my motives. But others do not. Help me be careful so I do not cause others to stumble, perhaps through misunderstandings or my poor example. Instead, may they see I am a sincere believer, imperfectly pointing them to You, praying they too will believe and follow Your example.

# November

# 23

## II CORINTHIANS 5:7–11

*We live by faith, not by sight. We are confident, I say, and would prefer to be away from the body and at home with the Lord. So we make it our goal to please him, whether we are at home in the body or away from it. For we must all appear before the judgment seat of Christ, that each one may receive what is due him for the things done while in the body, whether good or bad. Since, then, we know what it is to fear the Lord, we try to persuade men. What we are is plain to God, and I hope it is also plain to your conscience.*

Dear Lord,

I believe in You, I have faith in You; though I have not seen you with my physical eyes, I feel Your constant presence within my spirit. My most important goal is to please You, though I know I fail You too often. Praise God that in Your mercy You sent Your Son Jesus Christ so that when I am called before the Judgment Seat, I will be covered by His precious blood, shed for forgiveness of sin. May I live my life in such a way it is plain to those around me that I serve You, that I live differently—a life of purpose and truth, so they may be persuaded to follow You too.

# November

# 24

Dear Lord,

I know as Christians we are simply sinners saved by Your grace. Restrain me from committing acts that will once again make me a captive in the yoke of sin. Rather, make me a fit vessel for the indwelling of Your Holy Spirit. Make my life model Your righteousness before others lost in the cares of this world. May the light of Your love shine through me into their darkness; bring them into agreement with Your spiritual tugging on their hearts, setting them free to become one of Your Chosen people.

## II CORINTHIANS 6:14–16

*Do not be yoked together with unbelievers. For what do righteousness and wickedness have in common? Or what fellowship can light have with darkness? What harmony is there between Christ and Belial [Satan]? What does a believer have in common with an unbeliever? What agreement is there between the temple of God and idols? For we are the temple of the living God. As God has said: "I will live with them and walk among them, and I will be their God, and they will be my people."*

# November

# 25

## II CORINTHIANS 8:7, 10–12

*But just as you excel in every-thing—in faith, in speech, in knowledge, in complete earnestness and in your love for us—see that you also excel in this grace of giving. And here is my advice about what is best for you in this matter: Last year you were the first not only to give but also have the desire to do so. Now finish the work, so that your eager willingness to do it may be matched by your completion of it, according to your means. For if the willingness is there, the gift is acceptable accord-ing to what one has, not according to what he does not have.*

Dear Lord,

Sometimes I do not feel like I excel in anything, that I am of no use to myself, let alone You. Help me willingly give of what I have; show me what I excel in that You can use. Use my talents, my measure of faith, my speech, my knowledge base, my money, to be an encouragement to others. Thank you for reminding me that the willingness to give of myself rather than the volume of what I have to give is what matters.

# November

# 26

## EPHESIANS 4:1–6

Dear Lord,

I believe with all my heart, soul and mind You are the one true God. I believe in the three in One: God the Father, Son, and Holy Spirit—and our one hope is through Jesus Christ. You love each of us, our diversity attests to Your infinite imagination. I pray Your love and gentleness be manifest in me, helping me do my humble part in keeping unity of the Spirit here on earth while I await Your return.

*As a prisoner for the Lord, then, I urge you to live a life worthy of the calling you have received. Be completely humble and gentle; be patient, bearing with one another in love. Make every effort to keep the unity of the Spirit through the bond of peace. There is one body and one Spirit—just as you were called to one hope when you were called—one Lord, one faith, one baptism; one God and Father of all, who is over all and through all and in all.*

# November

# 27

## EPHESIANS 4:29–32

*Do not let any unwholesome talk come out of your mouths, but only what is helpful for building others up according to their needs, that it may benefit those who listen. And do not grieve the Holy Spirit of God, with whom you were sealed for the day of redemption. Get rid of all bitterness, rage and anger, brawling and slander, along with every form of malice. Be kind and compassionate to one another, forgiving each other, just as in Christ God forgave you.*

Dear Lord,

I feel justified in my attitude when I have been wronged and feel I am owed reparation. However, I do not want to grieve the Holy Spirit with my attitude. Therefore, despite difficult circumstances, please help me guard my tongue from unwholesome talk, my spirit from bitterness, my heart from malice. Help me forgive as You have forgiven; thank you my fate is sealed with Your Holy Spirit.

# November

## 28

Dear Lord,

Please give me a discerning spirit so I may understand Your will for me. Help me to be careful how I live—it is not an easy task. I need Your wisdom and light. The darkness can be so deep, and my light seems so dim. Help me remember it is not my light, rather Your light shining in me. Since I have accepted You in my heart You dwell in it, and are with me at all times, including in the darkness. You are the goodness, the righteousness and the truth—I need to let You shine forth to dispel the darkness for me and for those around me.

### EPHESIANS 5:8–17

*For you were once in darkness, but now you are light in the Lord. Live as children of light (for the fruit of the light consists in all goodness, righteousness and truth) and find out what pleases the Lord. Have nothing to do with the fruitless deeds of darkness, but rather expose them. For it is shameful even to mention what the disobedient do in secret. But everything exposed by the light becomes visible, for it is light that makes everything visible. This is why it is said: "Wake up, O sleeper, rise from the dead, and Christ will shine on you." Be very careful, then, how you live—not as unwise but as wise, making the most of every opportunity, because the days are evil. Therefore do not be foolish, but understand what the Lord's will is.*

# November

# 29

## PHILIPPIANS 2:4–11

*Each of you should look not only to your own interests, but also to the interests of others. Your attitude should be the same as that of Christ Jesus: Who, being in very nature God, did not consider equality with God something to be grasped, but made himself nothing, taking the very nature of a servant, being made in human likeness. And being found in appearance as a man, he humbled himself and became obedient unto death— even death on a cross! Therefore God exalted him to the highest place and gave him the name that is above every name, that at the name of Jesus every knee should bow, in heaven and on earth and under the earth, and every tongue confess that Jesus Christ is Lord, to the glory of God the Father.*

Dear Lord,

I do my best to follow Your example, and look not only to my own interests, but also to the interests of others. I use this guideline in my home, at work, with church activities and wherever else You may find me. Because my Lord was a servant on earth, I must be a servant also. It is a difficult path at times, especially when I am in need of some help myself, and there seems to be none forthcoming. However, You are my help. I am Your humble servant at all costs; for Your name alone do I bow on my knees, only to You may my tongue confess You are my Savior, Christ the Lord.

# November

# 30

Dear Lord,

I pray for Your will be done in my life, that I will continually grow in Your spiritual knowledge and understanding so I may be strengthened for the times when life does not turn out how I have planned. Help me know, no matter what, You are still the One in power; Your might and wisdom is above all others. Through the tough times as I wait for Your answers, please help me be patient and endure with Your strength, as my own is not enough. For I know deliverance will come, in Your way, in Your time.

## COLOSSIANS 1:9–12

*For this reason, since the day we heard about you, we have not stopped praying for you and asking God to fill you with the knowledge of his will through all spiritual wisdom and understanding. And we pray this in order that you may live a life worthy of the Lord and may please him in every way: bearing fruit in every good work, growing in the knowledge of God, being strengthened with all power according to his glorious might so that you may have great endurance and patience, and joyfully giving thanks to the Father, who has qualified you to share in the inheritance of the saints in the kingdom of light.*

# December

# 1

## COLOSSIANS 1:21–23

*Once you were alienated from God and were enemies in your minds because of your evil behavior. But now he has reconciled you by Christ's physical body through death to present you holy in his sight, without blemish and free from accusation—if you continue in your faith, established and firm, not moved from the hope held out in the gospel.*

Dear Lord,

It is hard to think of myself as an enemy of God. It is hard for me to sometimes understand that the God of Abraham and Moses in the Old Testament is the same God made flesh in Jesus Christ. Through Bible study, prayer and faith I have come to understand. God created us for His pleasure— the first commandment is to have no other gods before Him. If I am not living my life for Him, I am against Him, behaving like His enemy. In Old Testament times, only the Jews had access to God, and only through their prophets. Praise God, in the New Testament He sent His Son so that all may be His children through the Gospel of Jesus Christ. We have a direct link through the Holy Spirit—no priest or prophet or pastor required; we come to know Him through faith in His Word, hope in our prayers, and submission in our hearts.

# December

# 2

Dear Lord,

I do my best keeping my mind on what You want for my life. Sometimes, however, it is difficult to figure out Your plan. You are right, it is not hard to know that these things need to be left out of my life, but human nature lets some of them creep in, even when I'm trying to be so diligent. I pray You keep my life moral; may Your strength uphold me in my weakness. Keep me from greed, anger, and ugly words. Instead, keep me honest, soft-spoken, and speaking encouragement; let these things be my practice, that I may exemplify a moral, peaceful believer in Christ.

## COLOSSIANS 3:2–8

*Set your minds on things above, not on earthly things. For you died, and your life is now hidden with Christ in God. When Christ, who is your life, appears, then you also will appear with him in glory. Put to death, therefore, whatever belongs to your earthly nature: sexual immorality, impurity, lust, evil desires and greed, which is idolatry. Because of these, the wrath of God is coming. You used to walk in these ways, in the life you once lived. But now you must rid yourselves of all such things as these: anger, rage, malice, slander, and filthy language from your lips.*

# December

# 3

## COLOSSIANS
### 3:12–15

*Therefore, as God's chosen people, holy and dearly loved, clothe yourselves with compassion, kindness, humility, gentleness and patience. Bear with each other and forgive whatever grievances you may have against one another. Forgive as the Lord forgave you. And over all these virtues put on love, which binds them all together in perfect unity. Let the peace of Christ rule in your hearts, since as members of one body you were called to peace. And be thankful.*

Dear Lord,

Thank you for choosing me. Thank you for clothing me with Your calming virtues— let them prevail at all times, even under duress. Help me be forgiving, as You forgave me. May my willingness to forgive grievances give others the same tendency; rather, help us not grieve each other in the first place. As we follow Your Word, help us put the virtue of love above all others, so we may live in harmonious unity and the peace of Christ.

# December

COLOSSIANS 3:17, 23–24

*And whatever you do, whether in word or deed, do it all in the name of the Lord Jesus, giving thanks to God the Father through him ... Whatever you do, work at it with all your heart, as working for the Lord, not for men, since you know that you will receive an inheritance from the Lord as a reward. It is the Lord Christ you are serving.*

Dear Lord,

Thank you for this scripture. Work seems never ending, whether it be for the children, the home, the extended family, the church, the employer; my job descriptions are endless, and getting help or hearing 'thank you' is often scarce. Yet here in Your Word I find an answer to quiet my troubled soul. Your help is always just a prayer away. You have done so much for me; my salvation and eternal home are reward enough for any work I do. So when I put it into that perspective, that in all my work, whatever it is, I am serving the Lord, I willingly want to do my best with all my heart.

# December

# 5

## I THESSALONIANS
### 4:1–8

*Finally, brothers, we instructed you how to live in order to please God, as in fact you are living. Now we ask you and urge you in the Lord Jesus to do this more and more. For you know what instructions we gave you by the authority of the Lord Jesus. It is God's will that you should be sanctified: that you should avoid sexual immorality; that each of you should learn to control his own body in a way that is holy and honorable, not in passionate lust like the heathen, who do not know God; and that in this matter no one should wrong his brother or take advantage of him. The Lord will punish men for all such sins, as we have already told you and warned you. For God did not call us to be impure, but to live a holy life. Therefore, he who rejects this instruction does not reject man but God, who gives you his Holy Spirit.*

Dear Lord,

I pray I daily live my life to please You. May the words out of my mouth and the actions in my behavior show my profession of faith in Jesus Christ, and bring honor to Your name. May I practice self-control appropriately in all aspects of my behavior, be it intimate, financial, parenting, during conflicts, or any other situation where temptation presents itself, and I must make a choice to accept or reject Your instruction. I pray I will consistently choose Your way more and more as You lead me along life's journey.

# December

# 6

## 1 THESSALONIANS
4:11–12

*Make it your ambition to lead a quiet life, to mind your own business and to work with your hands, just as we told you, so that your daily life may win the respect of outsiders and so that you will not be dependent on anybody.*

Dear Lord,

It is my ambition to lead a quiet life and to do my best at the work you place before me. Sometimes, though, I know I use these ambitions to hide my deep-seated pain. I fill my life with busy-ness and responsibilities so I do not have time to reflect on the hurts in my heart. Thank you that I have gained the respect of others through the abilities You have given me. But help me not be dependent on them for my self-worth; help me depend only on You for value, only on You for instruction on how to live a life of value. I know it is You who has given me life and salvation; only through Your love can hurts be healed, forgiveness given, and lasting joy fill my heart.

# December

# 7

## I THESSALONIANS
5:14–22

*And we urge you, brothers, warn those who are idle, encourage the timid, help the weak, be patient with everyone. Make sure that nobody pays back wrong for wrong, but always try to be kind to each other and to everyone else. Be joyful always; pray continually; give thanks in all circumstances, for this is God's will for you in Christ Jesus. Do not put out the Spirit's fire; do not treat prophecies with contempt. Test everything. Hold on to good. Avoid every kind of evil.*

Dear Lord,

I am a patient person, I am kind, and I make every effort not to pay back wrong for wrong. However, I am having trouble giving thanks in all circumstances; my trials and heartache are larger than life, and I cannot see past them to a hopeful future. Please stoke the fire of Your Holy Spirit in mine—help me look around to all the daily blessings You provide in my life, regardless of my circumstances. Family, food, shelter, clothing, employment; fresh air, green grass, colorful flowers, the beauty of nature; my Bible, and the peace that passes understanding when I am alone in the quiet place to worship You. Yes, I can give thanks in all circumstances, because You are always there. May I be a yielded vessel to Your will in everything.

Dear Lord,

I lift up holy hands to worship You in submission, and I am in awe that You sent Your Son to live, die, and rise again for me. I pray the way I conduct my life is a testimony of Your worthiness and righteousness, including my attire. I will dress with decency, not using jewelry and clothes to call attention to my feminine shape, rather wearing those items in modesty and with proper grooming. This Scripture confuses me though, when it speaks of women should be silent. Thank you for reminding me we must read the whole of Your Word, and You show me where the Bible has women of God who taught, prophesied, and served faithfully. And though Eve was the first sinner, Adam was the second, and so it has continued throughout time. Then again in I Corinthians 11 Paul talks of propriety of worship, and reiterates it is Christ who is the head, not man, and that men and women are dependent on each other by His design. It is both men and women who must submit fully to God.

# December

# 8

## I TIMOTHY 2:8–14

*I want men everywhere to lift up holy hands in prayer, without anger or disputing. I also want women to dress modestly, with decency and propriety, not with braided hair or gold or pearls or expensive clothes, but with good deeds, appropriate for women who profess to worship God. A woman should learn in quietness and full submission. I do not permit a woman to teach or to have authority over a man; she must be silent. For Adam was formed first, then Eve. And Adam was not the one deceived; it was the woman who was deceived and became a sinner.*

# December

# 9

## 1 TIMOTHY 4:7–10

*Have nothing to do with godless myths and old wives' tales; rather, train yourself to be godly. For physical training is of some value, but godliness has value for all things, holding promise for both the present life and the life to come. This is a trustworthy saying that deserves full acceptance (and for this we labor and strive), that we have put our hope in the living God, who is the Savior of all men, and especially of those who believe.*

Dear Lord,

I do not want to be deceived by godless myths, the new age catchall which combines religions and claims all ways lead to god, nor any other well-meaning or deliberately misleading teachings about gods. You have trained me not only through listening to others who have read Your Word, but I read it for myself—I discern for myself through prayer and Bible Study the interpretation that is valid. Your Spirit testifies with mine what the truth is. My only hope for understanding and wisdom is in You, my Living God whose Son Jesus Christ is my Savior.

# December

# 10

Dear Lord,

Help me flee evil desires no matter what my age; I want to pursue Your better ways: righteousness, faith, love and peace. As Your servant, help me be self-controlled so I may avoid foolish arguments and needless quarrelling. I pray for common sense and divine discernment so I may live by Your Truths. I want my life to reflect Your kindness, teaching others Your Way by example; by being gentle when meeting opposition rather than resentful; and by letting the instruction of Your Word and Spirit guide me in how to respond effectively in all situations. For it is only through learning, living, and sharing Your Truths will we escape the devil's traps and schemes.

## II TIMOTHY 2:22–26

*Flee the evil desires of youth, and pursue righteousness, faith, love and peace, along with those who call on the Lord out of a pure heart. Don't have anything to do with foolish and stupid arguments, because you know they produce quarrels. And the Lord's servant must not quarrel; instead, he must be kind to everyone, able to teach, not resentful. Those who oppose him he must gently instruct, in the hope that God will grant them repentance leading them to a knowledge of the truth, and that they will come to their senses and escape from the trap of the devil, who has taken them captive to do his will.*

# December

# 11

## II TIMOTHY 3:1–5

*But mark this: There will be terrible times in the last days. People will be lovers of themselves, lovers of money, boastful, proud, abusive, disobedient to their parents, ungrateful, unholy, without love, unforgiving, slanderous, without self-control, brutal, not lovers of the good, treacherous, rash, conceited, lovers of pleasure rather than lovers of God—having a form of godliness but denying its power. Have nothing to do with them.*

Dear Lord,

I see the last days are upon us. These are terrible times we live in, much of it is because men and women love themselves more than they love God or they have no faith at all and their actions prove it. Many lack self-control, are brutal and treacherous with others, are completely without concern or love for their fellowman; all the awful things listed in this Scripture are present in our fallen world today. And though Christians try to have nothing to do with these sinful behaviors, they insidiously force themselves into our lives using our weak human nature. I pray first and foremost You prevent me from behaving in any of these self-serving, ungodly ways—keep my spirit humble before You. My heart's desire is to diligently walk in Your ways so others may see the sincere love of God living in my soul. Second, I pray for a discerning spirit, that I may always be on guard against these wicked ways in myself and others. I call upon Your Spirit to protect me from them, or walk me through the resulting painful valleys.

# December

# 12

## TITUS 2:11–14

*For the grace of God that brings salvation has appeared to all men. It teaches us to say "No" to ungodliness and worldly passions, and to live self-controlled, upright and godly lives in this present age, while we wait for the blessed hope—the glorious appearing of our great God and Savior, Jesus Christ, who gave himself for us to redeem us from all wickedness and to purify for himself a people that are his very own, eager to do what is good.*

Dear Lord,

You know I am eager to do what is good in Your sight. I pray for grace and guidance when the road is difficult and lonely. I know You are always with me, yet it is sometimes hard to feel Your presence in the troubles and distractions of the present age. Purify my heart and thoughts so I may live a godly life, secure in the knowledge it is Your strength which sustains me, I do not have to rely on my own. When I am tempted, bring to mind the cost of redemption, Your precious sacrifice on the cross, so I may fight hard to maintain self-control and not give in to worldly passions for a moments pleasure, rather maintain sight that I am the Lord's very own, and pure pleasure is in pleasing You.

# December

# 13

## TITUS 3:5B–8

*He saved us through the washing of rebirth and renewal by the Holy Spirit, whom he poured out on us generously through Jesus Christ our Savior, so that, having been justified by his grace, we might become heirs having the hope of eternal life. This is a trustworthy saying. And I want you to stress these things, so that those who have trusted in God may be careful to devote themselves to doing what is good. These things are excellent and profitable for everyone.*

Dear Lord,

Thank you for pouring Your Holy Spirit upon me, washing over me as the spring of Living Water; daily I thirst for Your renewal of my heart, mind and soul. Doing this is profitable not only for myself, but for those around me because I am devoted to doing good in Your Name. When I am discouraged, I need to remember first and foremost the blessing of salvation through Jesus Christ. Remind me that, no matter what else is going on around me, my final destination, eternity with my Lord, has been determined by Your grace. When I am stressed about things, I need to stress these things—I trust You to cleanse my soul, renew my strength, bestow grace sufficient for each day, and my hope is in You for all of my days. It is well with my soul.

# December

# 14

Dear Lord,

Encourage my heart today; I pray for a believing heart every day despite the life challenges trying to disillusion my faith. I sincerely want to hear and heed Your voice, so that through to the end I will hold firm that my confidence is in Christ alone. Let no sin creep in to deceive me, causing me to rebel. I pray for lasting obedience, nurtured by Your Truth that is imprinted upon my soul, which allows me to enter into Your rest.

## HEBREWS 3:12–19

*See to it, brothers, that none of you has a sinful, unbelieving heart that turns away from the living God. But encourage one another daily, as long as it is called Today, so that none of you may be hardened by sin's deceitfulness. We have come to share in Christ if we hold firmly till the end the confidence we had at first. As has just been said: "Today if you hear his voice, do not harden your hearts as you did in the rebellion." Who were they who heard and rebelled? Were they not all those Moses led out of Egypt? And with whom was he angry for forty years? Was it not with those who sinned, whose bodies fell in the desert? And to whom did God swear that they would never enter his rest if not to those who disobeyed? So we see that they were not able to enter, because of their unbelief.*

# December

# 15

### HEBREWS
### 12:14–15, 28–29

*Make every effort to live in peace with all men and to be holy; without holiness no one will see the Lord. See to it that no one misses the grace of God and that no bitter root grows up to cause trouble and defile many ... Therefore, since we are receiving a kingdom that cannot be shaken, let us be thankful, and so worship God acceptably with reverence and awe, for our "God is a consuming fire."*

Dear Lord,

As much as individuals want peace, it is an elusive state of being. Conflict amongst God's people is as common place as anywhere else: within Christian families, within churches, within relationships, all while doing God's work. I need to see to it I do not miss God's grace, I do not defile myself by letting bitter roots grow up and interfere with my purpose. My purpose is to worship You in truth and deed, to revere Your name, to bow in awe at Your feet because of Your mercy and love towards me. Make me holy, I pray, for Your glory.

# December

# 16

## HEBREWS
13:15–16, 20–21

Dear Lord,

I pray You will work in me what is pleasing to You. I gladly confess Your name on my lips, an easy sacrifice of praise. I try to do good things and share my Christian love through my attitude and work ethic. Though I am not an outspoken evangelistic type, I hope to softly influence others with my quiet gentle personality, and talk of You is part of my normal everyday conversation. Show me, I pray, how to do more to honor You with my life.

*Through Jesus, therefore, let us continually offer to God a sacrifice of praise—the fruit of lips that confess his name. And do not forget to do good and to share with others, for with such sacrifices God is pleased ... May the God of peace, who through the blood of the eternal covenant brought back from the dead our Lord Jesus, that great Shepherd of the sheep, equip you with everything good for doing his will, and may he work in us what is pleasing to him, through Jesus Christ, to whom be glory forever and ever. Amen.*

# December

# 17

## JAMES 1:19–22

*My dear brothers, take note of this: Everyone should be quick to listen, slow to speak and slow to become angry, for man's anger does not bring about the righteous life that God desires. Therefore, get rid of all moral filth and the evil that is so prevalent and humbly accept the word planted in you, which can save you. Do not merely listen to the word, and so deceive yourselves. Do what it says.*

Dear Lord,

Watching the world around me, with immorality firmly ensconced in our societal mainstream and the prevalence of evil behavior in the international community, as well as at home, it is hard to believe anyone is quick to listen, slow to speak and slow to anger. The media can make it all seem so hopeless. However, I read Your Word, seeking to know Your desire for my life. I humbly accept the hope it plants in my heart, that belief in You does make a difference, not just by listening to Your Word, but also doing what it says. I sincerely pray, please help me to continually strive to do what Your Word says.

# December

# 18

Dear Lord,

I like to help people, share my knowledge where it will benefit others. Thank you for reminding me that with knowledge comes responsibility and expectations. I must be thoughtful of what and how I say things, as I can not only lead myself but also others astray if I am careless. May You live in my heart, soul and mind, as I give myself to You each day, so what comes out of my mouth is obedient and serves Your purpose.

## JAMES 3:1–5A

*Not many of you should presume to be teachers, my brothers, because you know that we who teach will be judged more strictly. We all stumble in many ways. If anyone is never at fault in what he says, he is a perfect man, able to keep his whole body in check. When we put bits into the mouths of horses to make them obey us, we can turn the whole animal. Or take ships as an example. Although they are so large and are driven by strong winds, they are steered by a very small rudder wherever the pilot wants to go. Likewise the tongue is a small part of the body, but it makes great boasts.*

# December

# 19

## JAMES 3:5B–10

*Consider what a great forest is set on fire by a small spark. The tongue also is a fire, a world of evil among the parts of the body. It corrupts the whole person, sets the whole course of his life on fire, and is itself set on fire by hell. All kinds of animals, birds, reptiles and creatures of the sea are being tamed and have been tamed by man, but no man can tame the tongue. It is a restless evil, full of deadly poison. With the tongue we praise our Lord and Father, and with it we curse men, who have been made in God's likeness. Out of the same mouth come praise and cursing. My brothers, this should not be.*

Dear Lord,

Tame my tongue. May it be set on fire only in service for You. I do not want my life corrupted by thoughtless talk, rather I pray for You to set the course of my life, the proof being in Your wise words coming out of my mouth. Praise for Your blessings is often on my lips; and as Your Word commands, keep me from cursing and unkind conversation. Tame my tongue I pray.

# December

# 20

## JAMES 3:13–18

*Who is wise and understanding among you? Let him show it by his good life, by deeds done in the humility that comes from wisdom. But if you harbor bitter envy and selfish ambition in your hearts, do not boast about it or deny the truth. Such "wisdom" does not come down from heaven but is earthly, unspiritual, of the devil. For where you have envy and selfish ambition, there you find disorder and every evil practice. But the wisdom that comes from heaven is first of all pure; then peace-loving, considerate, submissive, full of mercy and good fruit, impartial and sincere. Peacemakers who sow in peace raise a harvest of righteousness.*

Dear Lord,

I am humble before You, desiring Your wisdom to lead me in a good life. Let my ambition be to do Your will at home and at work, at living orderly and faithfully in line with Your precepts: to love peace, be sincerely considerate of others as You are of me, and working towards producing good fruits for Your glory.

# December

# 21

## I PETER 1:13–17

*Therefore, prepare your minds for action; be self-controlled; set your hope fully on the grace to be given you when Jesus Christ is revealed. As obedient children, do not conform to the evil desires you had when you lived in ignorance. But just as he who called you is holy, so be holy in all you do; for it is written: "Be holy, because I am holy." Since you call on a Father who judges each man's work impartially, live your lives as strangers here in reverent fear.*

Dear Lord,

I often feel like a stranger in this world; alone, unnoticed, ignored, misunderstood. Yet my hope is in Your grace— when I call out my heavenly Father hears me, cares about me, loves me in spite of my shortcomings. May my mind and spirit be prepared to hear Your voice and follow Your lead. Help me live a life of obedience, striving for Your holiness. May it be obvious in my behavior that I desire to conform to Your image, disdaining the wickedness of this world.

# December

# 22

Dear Lord,

I pray for Your love to live in my heart so I may love others. May I crave the spiritual food of Your Word and continually learn of You. Show me my sinful nature, ferret out the hidden jealousy, any mean spirited thoughts, temptations to deceive, or judgment of others, when I myself can be guilty of grieving the Holy Spirit with sinful ways. It is my heart's desire to obey the Truth—for I have tasted and seen that the Lord, He is good.

## I PETER 1:22–23, 2:1–3

*Now that you have purified yourselves by obeying the truth so that you have sincere love for your brothers, love one another deeply, from the heart. For you have been born again, not of perishable seed, but of imperishable, through the living and enduring word of God … Therefore, rid yourselves of all malice and all deceit, hypocrisy, envy, and slander of every kind. Like newborn babies, crave pure spiritual milk, so that by it you may grow up in your salvation, now that you have tasted that the Lord is good.*

# December

# 23

## I PETER 2:11–15

*Dear friends, I urge you, as aliens and strangers in the world, to abstain from sinful desires, which war against your soul. Live such good lives among the pagans that, though they accuse you of doing wrong, they may see your good deeds and glorify God on the day he visits us. Submit yourselves for the Lord's sake to every authority instituted among men: whether to the king, as the supreme authority, or to governors, who are sent by him to punish those who do wrong and to commend those who do right. For it is God's will that by doing good you should silence the ignorant talk of foolish men.*

Dear Lord,

I do not want to be considered a hypocrite by unbelievers, saying one thing and doing another. Rather may I follow Your Spirit's leading to do good deeds, obey earthly authority, abstain from sinful behavior. When others look at my life, I pray they do not see a Sunday Christian. Instead, I pray they see a humble human, daily thankful for God's grace that saved a wretch like me.

# December 24

## 1 PETER 3:3–5

*Your beauty should not come from outward adornment, such as braided hair and the wearing of gold jewelry and fine clothes. Instead, it should be that of your inner self, the unfading beauty of a gentle and quiet spirit, which is of great worth in God's sight. For this is the way the holy women of the past who put their hope in God used to make themselves beautiful.*

Dear Lord,

For women especially, our present day society excessively values physical beauty. I feel so inadequate, insignificant against the Hollywood 'standard' that is a woman's yardstick. How can I feel valued in this world when I fall so short of its standard, even with the braided hair, gold jewelry and fine clothes? Thank you for telling me that the condition of my inner self is of much more value than that of the outer. Help me have a gentle and quiet spirit so much so that the inner beauty glows to the outside for Your glory.

# December

# 25

## 1 PETER 4:16–19

*However, if you suffer as a Christian, do not be ashamed, but praise God that you bear that name. For it is time for judgment to begin with the family of God; and if it begins with us, what will the outcome be for those who do not obey the gospel of God? And, "If it is hard for the righteous to be saved, what will become of the ungodly and the sinner?" So then, those who suffer according to God's will should commit themselves to their faithful Creator and continue to do good.*

Dear Lord,

If I must suffer, let me suffer as a committed Christian ought: continually praising You, following You, not giving up in despair, nor lashing out in anger and hatred towards those who have wronged me. Instead, may I continue to reflect upon Your goodness in my life. Your faithful goodness brought the Son of God to earth, born in a humble manger, arriving to save mankind from sin and eternal death. As I reflect on Your priceless gift celebrated today, I renew my commitment of love for my Creator, my Savior and my Lord.

# December

# 26

Dear Lord,

I want to walk as You do, my loving Savior. I want to have Your Word written on my heart, I want to have Your truth living in me, I want my strongest desire to be obeying Your commands. I do not want to lie to myself, saying I know all there is about being a follower of Christ. Your Truth is everlasting, Your knowledge and wisdom beyond man's understanding, how could I ever completely know You? I will love You completely, with all my heart and soul and mind because You first loved me.

## I JOHN 2:3–6

*We know that we have come to know him if we obey his commands. The man who says, "I know him," but does not do what he commands is a liar, and the truth is not in him. But if anyone obeys his word, God's love is truly made complete in him. This is how we know we are in him: Whoever claims to live in him must walk as Jesus did.*

# December

# 27

## 1 JOHN 3:23–24, 4:1–3A

*And this is his command: to believe in the name of his Son, Jesus Christ, and to love one another as he commanded us. Those who obey his commands live in him, and he in them. And this is how we know that he lives in us: We know it by the Spirit he gave us. Dear friends, do not believe every spirit, but test the spirits to see whether they are from God, because many false prophets have gone out into the world. This is how you can recognize the Spirit of God: Every spirit that acknowledges that Jesus Christ has come in the flesh is from God, but every spirit that does not acknowledge Jesus is not from God.*

Dear Lord,

My heart's desire is for the Lord Jesus Christ to dwell in my soul; I believe He is God's only Son, the only path to salvation. My heart's desire is to love others as You have commanded so I may live daily in Your presence. I pray for the gift of discernment so your Holy Spirit within me confirms the spiritual messages which acknowledge Jesus as the Son of God and the Son of Man. And may the discernment expose the watered-down versions of the Gospel that seek to deceive, offering false hope in a path to darkness without the Son.

# December

# 28

## I JOHN 5:3–8

*This is love for God: to obey his commands. And his commands are not burdensome, for everyone born of God overcomes the world. This is the victory that has overcome the world, even our faith. Who is it that overcomes the world? Only he who believes that Jesus is the Son of God. This is the one who came by water and blood—Jesus Christ. He did not come by water only, but by water and blood. And it is the Spirit who testifies, because the Spirit is the truth. For there are three that testify: the Spirit, the water and the blood; and the three are in agreement.*

Dear Lord,

Your commands are not burdensome, they are for my own good. Faith and following Your Word protects my soul and spirit from the worldly despair and hopelessness. Thank you for Your Spirit who gives me victory day after day over depression, over pain, over discouragement, over fear of the future. Thank you for the imagery in water baptism: going under, putting to death the old sinful self, emerging washed clean, symbolizing my commitment of following my Risen Lord in a Christian life. Thank You, Jesus, for your shed blood; it covers my forgiven sins with Your righteousness since I believe and accept You are the Messiah, the Savior of the world.

# December

# 29

## REVELATIONS 2:2–7

*I know your deeds, your hard work and your perseverance. I know that you cannot tolerate wicked men, that you have tested those who claim to be apostles but are not, and have found them false. You have persevered and have endured hardships for my name, and have not grown weary. Yet I hold this against you: You have forsaken your first love. Remember the height from which you have fallen! Repent and do the things you did at first. If you do not repent, I will come to you and remove your lampstand from its place. But you have this in your favor: You hate the practices of the Nicolaitans which I also hate. He who has an ear, let him hear what the Spirit says to the churches. To him who overcomes, I will give the right to eat from the tree of life, which is in the paradise of God.*

Dear Lord,

I test spiritual teachings against Your Word to ensure I am believing in the Truth. I endure hardships, but I grow weary from the battle. Lord, You know I need a brand-new touch. Fill me with Your Spirit as I was when I first loved You, the childlike trust when I first came to know where my Help comes from. Revive the devotion and faith I had when I was young and naïve; I have suffered, yet been blessed, overcoming so much since that little girl asked You into her heart. Fill my lamp again and again, so I am ready when You come for Your children. Please do not let me be like the Nicolaitans, who compromised their faith by mixing it with idolizing and practicing the immorality of this world. Rather may I hear Your gentle whispers, telling me the way in which to overcome the snares of this life, so I may reach God's paradise at the end of my days.

# December

# 30

## REVELATIONS
## 3:19–22

Dear Lord,

I am earnest, I repent, I know You are at my door, and I hold it wide open for You to enter and dwell within my soul. Yet there are times I do not overcome the trials before me, rather I am over run by the cares and hurts of this world. Help me understand whether the trials are Your loving rebuke to bring me back to Your path, or if they are just because we mortals dwell in an imperfect world. I know that someday this world will give way to an eternity with or without You. I see You, I know You are the Truth, I look for the day I will bow before Your Throne and be forever in fellowship with My Lord.

*Those whom I love I rebuke and discipline. So be earnest, and repent. Here I am! I stand at the door and knock. If anyone hears my voice and opens the door, I will come in and eat with him, and he with me. To him who overcomes, I will give the right to sit with me on my throne, just as I overcame and sat down with my Father on his throne. He who has an ear, let him hear what the Spirit says to the churches.*

# December

# 31

## REVELATIONS 22:7, 17–21

*Behold, I am coming soon! Blessed is he who keeps the words of the prophecy in this book ... The Spirit and the bride say, "Come!" And let him who hears say, "Come!" Whoever is thirsty, let him come; and whoever wishes, let him take the free gift of the water of life. I warn everyone who hears the words of the prophecy of this book: If anyone adds anything to them, God will add to him the plagues described in this book. And if anyone takes words away from this book of prophecy, God will take away from him his share in the tree of life and in the holy city, which are described in this book. He who testifies to these things says, "Yes, I am coming soon." Amen. Come, Lord Jesus. The grace of the Lord Jesus be with God's people. Amen.*

Dear Lord,

I await Your coming with faithful anticipation—knowing that in that day the cares of this world vanish forever in Your Holy Presence. Let the words of my mouth be true to Your Word; keep me thirsty for more of Your Truth, not adding or taking away from it, which may cause others to stumble or walk away from the eternal life you freely give. Come into our hearts to live; and when this world's end has come, return in triumph to take us home to heaven to be with You always.